# Alcoholics
# and Their Families

# Alcoholics and Their Families

## A GUIDE FOR CLERGY AND CONGREGATIONS

*John E. Keller*

📖 HarperSanFrancisco
*A Division of* HarperCollins*Publishers*

FIRST EDITION

This edition is printed on acid-free paper that meets the American National Standards Institute Z39.48 Standard.


**Library of Congress Cataloging-in-Publication Data**

Keller, John E.
  Alcoholics and their families / John E. Keller. — 1st ed.
        p.    cm.
  Includes bibliographical references.
  ISBN 0-06-064305-6 (alk. paper)
    1.   Church work with alcoholics.    2.  Alcoholics—Religious
  life.    3. Alcoholism.    4. Alcoholics—family relationships.
  I. title.
  Bv4460.5.K39 1991
  261.8'32292—dc20                                                    90-55294
                                                                           CIP

91   92   93   94   95   BG   10   9   8   7   6   5   4   3   2   1

To the memory of Dr. Nelson J. Bradley, considered to be the founder of modern-day alcoholism treatment programs, the person who suggested the idea of a specialized ministry in alcoholism.

# Contents

# Acknowledgments

I want to express my appreciation to Doreen Dionne for some of the early typing and special appreciation to Karen Cornforth, who evidenced extraordinary patience and endurance with a willing spirit in typing and retyping all the chapters.

# Preface

Statistics tell us that there are several million alcoholics in the United States and the world. Many people classified as alcoholics are also addicted to other drugs, including tranquilizers, sedatives, amphetamines, marijuana, cocaine, and crack. Alcohol is the only nonprescription or legal drug in this mix.

*Throughout history alcohol has been and continues to be the primary drug of choice.* Alcoholism is far and away the largest drug problem in congregations in our country and in the world. That is why, despite our knowledge of multiple addictions, alcohol and alcoholism are the primary focus of this book. Nonetheless, when you read the words "alcohol" and "alcoholism" in this book, *know that all of the other listed drugs are included in the broader spectrum of drug addiction.*

You may be surprised that alcohol is identified here as a drug. Frequently, we read or hear the phrase "alcohol and drugs" rather than "alcohol and other drugs," and we are all aware of the serious drug problem in our society. But other drug addictions singularly and in combination have never come close in numbers to alcohol addiction.

These are the statistics: sixty percent or more of youth and adults in mainline Protestant nonprohibitionist churches drink alcoholic beverages. Ninety-two percent of high school seniors have tried alcohol; 64 percent of high school seniors have used alcohol in the last month; 35 percent of high school seniors get drunk once a week; 6 percent of high school seniors are daily drinkers; 38 percent of high school sophomores get drunk a couple of times a month, as do 26 percent of eighth graders. The average beginning age of alcohol use is twelve and a half years.[1]

Most people who drink will not end up with a drinking problem; but one out of ten or twelve will. That percentage also applies to pastors and their spouses. The prohibitionist churches will have fewer drinkers; but among those who drink, a higher percentage will become alcoholics.

This means that in a congregation of five hundred youth and adult members of which 60 percent drink, there may be twenty-five to thirty alcoholics. If we multiply that figure by an average of four to include family members, who are identified as code-pendents, we have one hundred to one hundred and twenty people who need help. These people range from early teens to older adults, and come from all economic levels and vocations. They are both male and female—30 to 40 percent of alcoholics are women.

In this book we will look at what pastors and congregations need to know about alcoholism, and what they can do to help their alcoholic members. Right now, knowledgeable pastors and model programs exist in many congregations. Good literature, films, treatment programs—both outpatient and inpatient—and other resources are readily available. Linking the internal resources within the congregation with the external resources in the community will enable many to find freedom from the bondage of addiction and with that, hope, healing, new meaning, and fulfillment in life.

Because of the nature of the Christian faith and fellowship, this book also explores another question. Given the nature of our mutual brokenness, pain, limitation, and vulnerability, how do we identify within ourselves and our own behaviors that which has found expression in alcoholism in these people's lives? Surely, that is what was missing in the story of the Pharisee in the temple (Luke 18:9–14). He couldn't make the connection with the publican. In reality, this book is not only about alcoholics and their families. It is about all of us who confess our faith in Jesus Christ.

# Alcoholics
and Their Families

# 1. What Is Alcoholism?

Most people agree that alcoholism brings with it increasingly serious problems that affect the whole of a person's life, relationships, and responsibilities. But when they try to describe what causes alcoholism and what it's all about, the issue becomes confused. We encounter many definitions and descriptions of alcoholism: some are scientific and complex, others are unscientific and simplistic, still others are moralistic and judgmental.

In this book we will look for answers to that question in ways that are clinical, behavioral, nonmoralistic, and easy to comprehend. We will see that in its most basic definition, alcoholism is characterized by the inability of the drinker to control his or her drinking. We can begin to understand the scope of the problem within the context of four basic kinds of drinking: social drinking, drinking to drunkenness, problem (symptomatic) drinking, and alcoholism.

## SOCIAL DRINKING

The majority of youth and adults who drink will not end up as alcoholics but as what we commonly call social drinkers. Social drinkers drink for a variety of reasons, in varying amounts and varying frequency. Some only have a drink for toasts or on special occasions. Some drink infrequently. Some drink daily or a few days a week. Usually, but not always, social drinkers drink moderate amounts—one or two drinks. At certain times and places some may drink to a "mild euphoria." Occasionally, some social drinkers drink to drunkenness.

Social drinkers are not limited to beer and wine. Many social drinkers regularly or occasionally drink hard liquor and mixed drinks. Some drink only beer, or only wine, or only hard liquor, and some drink a variety of these, depending on the time, the occasion, and their desire.

Social drinkers are in control of their drinking. According to our definition, then, a social drinker does not drive if he or she is legally drunk because that is an accepted personal responsibility. People who drive while impaired by alcohol are not social drinkers, because they are being clearly irresponsible.

Social drinkers have their drinking integrated into their lives. They don't see drinking as something different or special or as necessary for social acceptance. Social drinkers don't get together just to drink. They feel free not to drink at given times, places, and occasions. They feel free to modify the frequency or amount of their alcohol consumption. For them a good time does not always mean having something to drink. They affirm those who choose abstinence and make sure non-alcoholic beverages are available for them.

Within the context of the Christian faith, social drinkers believe alcoholic beverages are among God's good gifts for the enhancement and enjoyment of life. They believe Jesus drank wine and in his first miracle created special wine when the guests had drunk all the wine provided at the wedding in Cana (John 2:1–11). Some within the Christian community, both church denominations and individuals, believe that any alcohol consumption is unacceptable according to the Christian faith. Despite this strong disagreement we can still have mutual respect for one another and common concern for alcoholics and their families.

According to our definition social drinkers are not alcoholics. Social drinkers drink the way they do, in frequency and in amount, within and according to their intention and by free choice.

## DRINKING TO DRUNKENNESS

Some drinkers drink to drunkenness—not just mild euphoria, but what is commonly called "getting drunk"—rarely, occasionally, or frequently. These are people who have the freedom and ability to drink and not get drunk if they so choose. Their drunkenness is intentional and willful. It happens because they want it to happen. For example:

- Joe knows on Monday that he is going to Bill's farewell party Friday evening. He already knows that he is going to drink to drunkenness. The following weekend he is going to another party, and his wife and children will be with him. At that party he has decided that he will drink, but not get drunk.

- Mary and her boyfriend have a few beers every day after work. On Friday nights they get together with their friends, and sometimes they decide to overdrink. When they wake up hung over or feeling some minor effects from overdrinking, they aren't surprised. They decided to overdrink and pay the price.

Some younger people choose to drink this way occasionally and frequently in high school and college. They are putting themselves at risk for developing an alcohol problem, but many of them will leave behind that basic drinking pattern as they move into their adult years.

For these people excessive drinking is within and according to their intention and by free choice. Since the Bible speaks of moderation in all things, this kind of drinking is clearly not within God's intention or will for us.

## PROBLEM (SYMPTOMATIC) DRINKING

Some social drinkers, who may never have drunk to drunkenness, may begin drinking symptomatically at a particularly difficult time. They seek the sedative effect of alcohol to escape from the real or perceived problems and pain in their lives. This is called problem drinking.

- Beth, a wife and mother, has for many years been heavily invested in her children for her own sense of personal identity, worth, and meaning. She has also been very active in the church, teaching Sunday school and belonging to a women's group. Her youngest child has now left home, and she feels a profound sense of loss and aloneness together with a diminished sense of personal identification, worth, and meaning. Beth has been a social drinker all her adult life. In her pain she finds herself alone at home taking a drink, and then another drink, to sedate the pain. She begins to drink more alcohol with her husband before dinner, and at get-togethers with friends. Although she doesn't really let herself know what she is doing, she has clearly become a symptomatic problem drinker and could be in the early stages of alcoholism.

• George and Mary have been social drinkers all their adult years. He has recently retired, and they have moved into a senior-citizen trailer-home park in Arizona. They remain active in the church, but time weighs heavy during the day. They begin to have their before-dinner cocktails with friends in the trailer park at a much earlier hour, and inevitably they increase their drinking. After a while Mary becomes aware of what is happening. She talks to George about it, saying she wants to go back to their regular pattern. George's response is irritable and argumentative. He ignores the danger signal Mary has seen. He is into problem drinking. He clearly is drinking now *primarily* for relief and could already be an alcoholic.

• Carol is a young wife and mother. She and her husband, Rick, scheduled an evaluation of her drinking at an alcoholism facility because her drinking had become problematic. As she told her story to the counselor, it was clear that she was depressed after experiencing the loss of her mother, with whom she had been very close. The counselor thought that her drinking was possibly symptomatic, not yet alcoholism. Although alcoholism can produce depression, her drinking hadn't evolved to that stage in the alcoholism progression. She was referred to a psychiatrist who was a specialist in alcoholism to continue to assess the drinking. Over time Carol worked through her grief and the problematic drinking ceased.

Beth and George still have freedom of choice and the ability to either quit drinking that way or quit drinking altogether. They may come to the realization, as Mary did, that what they are doing is no longer social drinking. They may look for ways to get involved and be of service, quit drinking altogether, seek help for their problems, or simply come to the point where they can and do let go of that kind of relief drinking.

Carol was fortunate that her family was able to bring her for treatment at this early stage. Women, perhaps because they suffer more intense shame and guilt, progress to alcoholism much more quickly than men. A significantly high percentage of problem drinkers become alcoholics, but not all. Clinical experience does indicate that by the time people become concerned enough to seek a professional assessment, the chances are very high that they may already be alcoholics.

Again, the primary factor in problem or symptomatic drinking in relationship to alcoholism is the existence of freedom of choice and the ability to discontinue the problem drinking or stop drinking altogether. If problem drinking continues, however, it is likely to become alcoholism.

## ALCOHOLISM

Alcoholism includes drinking, drinking to drunkenness, and problem drinking, but it is something different and more than either of these. What, then, is alcoholism?

The mark of alcoholism is loss of control: the inability or lack of freedom to drink within and according to one's own intention, in spite of increasing problems related to the drinking. Alcoholism is the inability to predictably and with consistency stay within moderate limits. Despite anything you have read or heard, once a person's drinking has passed into loss of control, *there is no way back to social drinking,* that is, to drinking in moderation within intention and by choice.

I have never known an alcoholic who, before taking the first drink, ever with intention and by choice decided to get drunk. The only exception is the skid-row alcoholic, and this is only 4 percent or 5 percent of all alcoholics. The vast majority of alcoholics intend only to have a few drinks. Their addiction prevents them from seeing that the recent or lengthy history of their alcoholic drinking has clearly demonstrated that they can't drink within and according to that intention.

The key phrase in this understanding of alcoholism, valida-
ted over and over again in Alcoholics Anonymous and clinical
experience, is "inability to drink within and according to one's
own intention." The freedom and ability to choose is perma-
nently gone. That's the essential difference between alcoholism and social drinking, drinking to drunkenness, and problem drinking. That is the bondage of alcoholism. The person has
neither the power nor the ability to quit or control the
drinking.

This also means the person doesn't have the individual power
or ability to keep from taking the first drink after a period of
abstinence. He or she needs outside help—including the help of
God, whether so recognized or not—to become free to stay away
from the first drink. Alcoholics Anonymous (AA) has as the first
Step for recovery, "Admitted we were powerless over alcohol
and our lives had become unmanageable." There is no better
description of alcoholism.

Loss of control is not only permanent, it is also predictably
progressive. If the loss of control does not initially involve all of
the drinking, it eventually will.

Catherine, a middle-aged wife and mother was concerned
about some, but not all, of her drinking. She and her husband
scheduled an evaluation. She could still drink socially with her
husband and friends. She enjoyed and wanted to continue that
kind of drinking. In recent months, however, she had started to
drink alone in the afternoon and was not in good condition
when her children and husband came home. She had tried to
change and stop that, but with no success. Catherine was diagnosed as having loss of control and being in the early stages of
alcoholism. She was told that she needed help and that, if she
didn't get help, that kind of drinking would progressively take
over more and eventually all of her drinking.

An alcoholic said it well: "I used to be a problem drinker and
then I ended up with a drinking problem—alcoholism." In this
understanding of alcoholism, you can't be a little bit alcoholic.
You either have alcoholism or you don't. If you have alcoholism,
whether in the early, middle, or late stages, you need outside
help. Fortunately, more alcoholics and their families are seeking
help earlier in this progression.

Some people lose control over their drinking from their very first drink. As they relate their drinking histories, receive education on alcoholism, or talk with professional staff and other patients, they become aware that their drinking was never normal or social. They always drank as much as was available. They always got drunk. Frequently, they have a history of high tolerance, commonly described as the ability to "drink anyone under the table." High tolerance, as we shall see later, is a danger signal that alcoholism may be ahead.

Alcoholism is also progressive in another way. The out-of-control drinking, with its increased frequency and duration, will cause increasing problems in every area of the person's life: physical, mental, emotional, social, vocational, and spiritual. The end result of all untreated alcoholism is either permanent brain damage or death.

This understanding of alcoholism raises other questions: Why do one out of ten or twelve who drink experience loss of control? Why doesn't this happen to all drinkers? No one has the answer to that question. Some people have sought to prove a psychological cause or personality type, and have identified what they believe are personality traits of alcoholics; but there are people with those traits who drink and don't become alcoholics. Certainly, there is a higher incidence of alcoholism in families with an alcoholic parent or parents. Such a family history may be part of the cause, but certainly isn't all of it. Recent research has identified genetic factors that may be proven to be causative in these families, particularly with early onset. Sociologists believe alcoholism is caused by multiple factors.

A more critical question for the church is, What about the moral responsibility related to drinking and the excessive drinking that leads to alcoholism? This question has never been sufficiently addressed, either by professionals in alcoholism treatment or by the church. It would seem clear that the question of whether the alcoholic can be held morally responsible has to be answered affirmatively. At some point most, if not all, alcoholics had the freedom to quit drinking excessively and problematically, or to quit drinking altogether. Although there are no statistics on how many have done that, most of us know people who did.

However, if we know ourselves at all, we know the amazing capacity we have to deny or deceive ourselves about the signs of a developing drinking problem or any other problem. Those who had obvious danger signals but didn't see them, or who ignored them or denied them on their way to alcoholism, should not be blamed by those within the church who are social drinkers or who don't drink at all. Wearing blinders to the obvious and denying our problems are common, mutual behaviors.

On the question of moral responsibility, one point is of primary interest and importance: I have never met a recovering alcoholic who used the belief that alcoholism is a disease marked by loss of control as an exemption from personal responsibility for the alcoholism or for the recovery. Rather, after accepting their powerlessness over alcohol and their inability to free themselves from their bondage, recovering alcoholics come to accept responsibility for their condition and to seek help outside themselves to find freedom to remain abstinent. Through a spiritual recovery program, they find healing with new meaning and fulfillment in their lives by the grace of God.

Strange as it may sound, alcoholism serves as a paradigm of the human condition and a profound spiritual quest. As we seek our own personal identification with these people on our mutual journey with brokenness, pain, vulnerability, and human limitation, we can see more clearly our own behaviors of denial and deception in our own spiritual quest.

# 2. Progressive Symptoms of Alcoholism

Alcoholism is marked by a downward progression of destructive symptoms during active drinking and an upward progression of healthy behaviors in recovery. Early in the history of our contemporary understanding of alcoholism, Dr. E. M. Jellinek, a pioneer in alcohol studies, devised the Jellinek Chart to illustrate this progression. Variations of this chart, as shown in Figure 1, are widely used today in education and treatment programs.[1]

This chart describes the progressive symptoms of alcoholism and the progressive recovery markers, which Jellinek identified primarily from members of Alcoholics Anonymous. In his book *The Disease Concept of Alcoholism,* Dr. Jellinek later described five types of alcoholism, only one of which matches the Jellinek Chart.[2] This particular type he called Gamma alcoholism, the primary type of alcoholism in the United States and therefore the primary type of alcoholism addressed in this book.

The Jellinek Chart shows the insidious downward progression in every aspect of the person's life as the drinking progressively worsens. A parallel progression occurs in the lives of the family members, a situation we will explore in a later chapter.

A person may not experience all the symptoms. Many will experience most. But the basic progressive *pattern* is predictable, no matter who the person is. Even professionals in the field of alcoholism, in spite of their knowledge about the symptoms, experience and live them out if their drinking becomes alcoholism. Knowledge about the symptoms doesn't prevent denial of the symptoms.

Included in this progressive symptomatology is the predictable phenomenon of the person becoming locked into and blinded to

# The Progression
# and Recovery of the Alcoholic
# in the Disease of Alcoholism

*To be read from left to right.*

**Progression**

Occasional Relief Drinking

Constant Relief Drinking Commences

Increase in Alcohol Tolerance

Onset of Memory Blackouts

Surreptitious Drinking

Increasing Dependence on Alcohol

Unable to Discuss Problem

Decrease of Ability to Stop
Drinking When Others Do So

Urgency of First Drinks

Feelings of Guilt

Memory Blackouts Increase

Drinking Bolstered with Excuses

Grandiose and Aggressive Behavior

Efforts to Control Fail Repeatedly

Tries Geographical Escapes

*Crucial Phase*

Persistent Remorse

Promises and Resolutions Fail

Loss of Other Interests

Work and Money Troubles

Unreasonable Resentments

Neglect of Food

Physical Deterioration

Family and Friends Avoided

Loss of Ordinary Willpower

Tremors and Early-Morning Drinks

Decrease in Alcohol Tolerance

Onset of Lengthy Intoxications

Moral Deterioration

Impaired Thinking

Drinking with Inferiors

Indefinable Fears

Unable to Initiate Action

Obsession with Drinking

Vague Spiritual Desires

All Alibis Exhausted

Complete Defeat Admitted

*Chronic Phase*

Obsessive Drinking Continues
in Vicious Circles

Enlightened and Interesting Way of
Life Opens Up with Road Ahead to
Higher Levels than Ever Before.

Group Therapy and Mutual Help Continue

Rationalizations Recognized

Care of Personal Appearance

First Steps Toward Economic Stability

Increase of Emotional Control

Facts Faced with Courage

New Circle of Stable Friends

Family and Friends
Appreciate Efforts

Natural Rest and Sleep

Realistic Thinking

Regular Nourishment Taken

*Recovery*

Increasing Tolerance

Contentment in Sobriety

Confidence of Employers

Appreciation of Real Values

Rebirth of Ideals

New Interests Develop

Adjustment to Family Needs

Desire to Escape Goes

Return of Self-Esteem

Diminishing Fears of the Unknown Future

Appreciation of Possibilities of New Way of Life

Start of Group Therapy

Onset of New Hope

Physical Overhaul by Doctor

Spiritual Needs Examined

Right Thinking Begins

Takes Stock of Self

Meets Normal and Happy Former Addicts

Stops Taking Alcohol

Told Addiction Can Be Arrested

Learns Alcoholism is an Illness

Honest Desire for Help

*Rehabilitation*

the symptoms of an obvious drinking problem. Education and various types of intervention have made it possible for some people to have the blinders removed earlier in the progression than was true years ago, but the bondage of loss of control and denial go hand in glove.

## WARNING SIGNALS

The first set of symptoms or behaviors are warning signals. Like the highway sign that warns "Curve Ahead," these symptoms say "Warning—Possible Alcoholism Ahead." We include some that are not in the chart that have been identified through clinical experience and some that are more specific than those in the chart. *Any of these early symptoms in combination with another is a clear signal to recommend an assessment by an alcoholism professional.*

*Drinking more frequently.*

Drinking more frequently, taken alone, may not be significant. This type of change may be brought about by having more money to spend on alcohol, or becoming part of a social group that drinks more regularly than the person has in the past. This can still be social drinking as described in chapter 1.

*Increase in amount drunk in these more frequent drinking episodes.*

Again, this may not be significant if the amount is increased from one drink to two drinks on occasion. Frequently, however, there is a pattern of increased intake, which may mean the drinker is directly seeking more of the sedative effect of alcohol and developing increasing dependency.

*Neglecting to measure the amount of alcohol in a drink.*

When the person just pours alcohol out of the bottle into the glass, instead of using a jigger to measure, it usually means more alcohol is being consumed in each drink. Another person may fail to be mindful of the number of beers drunk or the number of glasses of wine drunk. Both are changes in the pattern of drinking. Any such change, and particularly in combination with other changes, constitutes a major warning signal.

*Drinking to relieve tension.*

Clearly, the above kinds of changes may signal that the person is beginning to drink primarily to relieve tension. A social drinker may do that on occasion. But when you begin to hear the words "I need a drink" with any kind of regularity, or the *pattern* of amount and frequency indicates drinking to relieve tension, there has been a significant change. This is problem drinking, because the person is now, with increased regularity, taking a drug in the midst of a personal problem or negative feeling.

*Increase in tolerance.*

An increase in tolerance is significant alone, and even more so in combination with any of the above warning signals. Tolerance is the need to drink more to get the same previous effect, and the ability to tolerate the increased intake. The presence of high tolerance at the beginning of a person's drinking or the evidence of developing increased tolerance are clear clinical indicators of problem drinking. "Being able to drink anyone under the table" was once commonly held to be macho. The fact is that such high tolerance early on in drinking can be a real warning signal of alcoholism.

*Sneaking Drinks*

Drinking before an event is followed by drinking the same or more than usual at the event. Doubles are mixed or ordered instead of singles. The person desires more alcohol. When this becomes a pattern, you have a serious warning signal and the drinking very likely is already alcoholism.

*The desire to continue drinking when others have stopped.*

The person who has this desire might mix a drink, maybe a double, just before guests are being seated for dinner. The double makes it another form of sneaking. The desire to continue drinking also might include not wanting to go home from a party as long as more drinking is possible.

*Being uncomfortable or less interested in social situations in which there will be no alcoholic drinks.*

This is a significant change, an indicator of problem drinking.

*Preoccupation with alcohol.*

Preoccupation has to do with thinking about drinking while at work or at home, say at mid-afternoon. The person who is preoccupied starts to watch the clock at work to see how long it will be before the workday is done and drinking can begin. Or this person may sit at home watching the clock, because five o'clock means cocktails. Drinking is increasingly associated with "feeling good," "having a good time," or "experiencing relief."

*Gulping drinks.*

Some people gulp their food and whatever they drink. If their drinking is not a problem, such gulpers will quit after a one or two drinks. However, gulping alcoholic drinks is never a good practice. Gulping becomes a warning signal when the person changes from sipping to gulping to get a desired effect sooner and to drink more than others are drinking. This is the person at a party whose glass is always empty when others haven't finished their drinks.

*Blackouts.*

The person who blacks out does not necessarily pass out; he or she experiences frightening loss of memory while conscious. Have you ever heard someone say, "I have no idea how I got home," or "I can't remember a thing that happened at the party"? That's a blackout. Some drinkers who have had a blackout are not alcoholics; some alcoholics have never had a blackout. But there is a high incidence of blackouts in alcoholism.

Blackouts can last from a few minutes to a few days, and there is usually no behavior to indicate severe intoxication. For example, a priest of a large parish who received a commendation from his bishop for his annual report could not recall ever doing the report. A man attended out-of-town meetings for three days and could not remember anything that went on. Both were alcoholics. Many hit-and-run accidents happen during blackouts.

Experiencing even one blackout is cause for real concern about a person's drinking. Two blackouts definitely means the person needs an assessment by an alcoholism professional.

*Irritation when someone raises questions about the person's drinking.*

The questioning means there has been a clear change in the drinking that is seen as problematic. Deep inside, the drinker may wonder but doesn't want to face it. The irritation is a sign of feeling guilty about drinking while denying a change in the drinking.

The original Jellinek Chart lists these warning signals above the loss of control line. They are indicators of what is described as problem drinking in chapter 1. However, if two or more of these drinking behaviors are present, there needs to be a professional assessment for alcoholism. If two or more have become a *pattern*, the chances are high that alcoholism is already present.

## LOSS OF CONTROL

Jellinek's Gamma alcoholism has four key characteristics: (1) acquired increased tissue tolerance to alcohol; (2) adaptive cell metabolism; (3) withdrawal symptoms and "craving," that is, physical dependence; and (4) loss of control. According to Jellinek this type of alcoholism creates the greatest and most serious kinds of damage.[3]

Loss of control is the definitive marker of Gamma alcoholism, and it brings with it the predictable deteriorating progression in all aspects of the person's life. Not all alcoholics experience the progressive symptoms, nor do they necessarily experience them in the order in which they are listed here. However, their pattern will include many, if not all, of the following symptoms.

*Rationalizing and alibiing the drinking.*

This is not only alcoholic behavior, it is common human behavior. We use it to keep the truth about ourselves from ourselves. It is as old as Adam and Eve: "It wasn't me, it was the woman you gave me." "It wasn't me, it was the serpent." *If drinking isn't a problem, there is no need to rationalize the drinking.* It is as simple as that.

What happens with loss of control, which no one wants to see or admit, is that *the rationalizing and alibiing become systematized.*

The person gets locked into this behavior, which includes the belief that the rationalizations are reality. With this comes lying about the drinking. Underneath this rationalization and alibi system, the person unconsciously harbors the idea that somehow, someday, he or she will be able to gain control of the drinking. This becomes the great obsession of the alcoholic—to drink with control. When that increasingly fails, creating further problems, the goal becomes to quit by one's own determination. The person thinks, "I can take it or leave it," unaware that the explanation for the overdrinking is now loss of control.

*Increase in frequency of relief drinking and sneaking drinks, with increased dependence on alcohol.*

The person is more interested in the alcohol than in drinking. Drinking has a new primary focus—alcohol ingestion. This means that even though the person may be drinking in social situations, he or she is in a real sense drinking alone. The drinker usually has no conscious awareness that the drinking has dramatically changed because by now denial has become entrenched.

*Guilt about the drinking.*

The person experiences guilt not only about drinking too much and related damaging behavior, but also because the drinking is "different" from that of family members and friends. The person quickly responds to the guilt with the elaborate rationalization and alibi system and by more drinking.

*Inability to discuss the problem.*

Efforts by family members to discuss what is now a drinking problem result in failure. The alcoholic's lack of awareness of loss of control, the rationalization and alibi system, and the projection of the problem onto family members, job, or another cause, result in arguments and blaming. Family members never win; they end up with more resentment and usually more guilt.

*Behavioral changes.*

*Morning tremors* or *inside jitters* are withdrawal effects that the alcoholic self-medicates with alcohol, tranquilizers, or both. Both the alcoholic and family members may express concern about this behavior, and the alcoholic may make all kinds of promises and resolutions about stopping the drinking. The alcoholic may sincerely mean and believe these promises, but loss of control prevents them from being kept.

*Lying about the drinking* progressively turns the drinker into a *dishonest person. Grandiose behaviors* may develop, such as playing the big shot and buying drinks for others while bills are going unpaid. *Aggressive behaviors* may also develop, such as becoming verbally and physically abusive while drunk.

*Changing the pattern of drinking.*

Changing the time or type of alcoholic drink is another attempt to solve the problem. The alcoholic may decide to stop going to a certain bar, to switch from hard liquor to beer, to drink only on weekends, or never to drink alone. None of these work, because they can't work.

*Family and friendship relationships deteriorate.*

Drinking companions change, so the person drinks with people who are drinking in the same way. The deterioration and loss of relationships is handled by rationalization and blaming. The person either does not recognize the change in drinking companions, or handles it by perceiving the previous social drinking friends as becoming snobbish. The drinker fails to see that the new drinking companions are not real friends, but only drinking friends.

*Guilt and remorse become more persistent.*

Self-condemnation multiplies the guilt feelings and more drinking anesthetizes them. This cycling phenomenon feeds into and speeds up the downward progression.

*Drinking begins to create serious job problems and even job loss.*

The alcoholic may quit a job before getting fired. In spite of the fact that drinking is endangering his or her source of income, the pathological drinking continues. Fortunately, many companies have employee assistance programs to enable referral for help related to job performance problems.

At this phase in the progression, a more rapid development of very serious problems begins. These can include *drinking alone and more obsessively, poor nutrition, physical deterioration, impairment in thinking, increasing and more disruptive family problems,* and *possible loss of family.* Chronic brain damage requiring institutionalization, or *death* as a result of irreversible physical deterioration, may be the final results of untreated alcoholism.

Two types of physical and mental damage are caused by alcoholism: acute and chronic. Acute means that the damage to the liver or brain, for instance, will repair and heal if the drinking ceases. Chronic means that the damaged part of the liver or brain will not repair or only mildly repair over a lengthy period of time of abstinence with good medical care and nutrition. Acute and chronic damage can be diagnosed with medical and psychological tests and clinical assessments. Hypertension and diabetes are common in alcoholism. Hypertension in the earlier phases of alcoholism can disappear with abstinence.

The social, psychological, and spiritual deterioration is readily seen in this progression. Faith in God and relationship to the church get swallowed up in resentment, guilt, shame, increasing sense of aloneness, and what becomes a pathological dishonesty. Prayers of desperation coupled with promises to quit drinking lead only to further disillusionment. Toward the end of the progression, the alcoholic is living to drink and drinking to live.

What we will describe in the next chapter as a spiritual quest for identity, healing, and meaning has resulted in literally losing one's life. It is difficult to imagine a more dramatic paradigm of losing life by seeking to save one's life than the progression of alcoholism. It parallels Jesus' story of the son who left his father's house and ended up bankrupt in every area of his life (Luke 15:11–32). Interestingly, recovering alcoholics find out that the answer for that son is also the answer for them.

# 3. The Spiritual Quest in Alcoholism

Our society seems to have become much more hedonistic in recent years. Our acceptance and tolerance for people getting drunk, getting stoned on marijuana, and, until recently, getting high on cocaine or crack to escape any kind of pain is a major change. From this it is possible to assume that more people become addicted to alcohol and other drugs just from taking too much for too long. This could be called "hedonistic alcoholism."

For most alcoholics, however, hedonism is not the pathway into alcoholism. *For most alcoholics alcohol provided an exceptional positive internal experience related to their human brokenness, pain, and vulnerability that is very different from the experience of the majority of people who drink.*

## THE TRANSFORMING EFFECT OF ALCOHOL FOR ALCOHOLICS

Many people who drink feel a sense of slight euphoria; but the mild anesthetic effect of alcohol does not transform their perception of themselves or their feelings about themselves and others and life itself. When you listen carefully to stories of alcoholics, however, you generally hear something very different. Many experienced from alcohol a rather immediate transforming effect. They didn't initially experience only the common "high"; they experienced an "unusual high." They experienced a sense of healing and wholeness and belonging. They thought this "magical" effect was experienced by all who drank, but most who drink don't know what it feels like to experience what the alcoholic feels from the effect of alcohol.

Why some people experience this special kind of effect no one yet knows. Maybe that is related to the genetic factor. Some people experience just the opposite effect. They get depressed and anxious from the effects of alcohol. Their chances of becoming alcoholic are slim indeed. One woman said to me, "If alcohol had worked for me, I know that I would have become an alcoholic." A colleague once said, "I tried alcohol, but it didn't work. I was stuck with being a depressive."

In the early years of my training at Willmar State Hospital in Willmar, Minnesota, where Dr. Nelson J. Bradley and his colleagues were putting together what became the model for modern-day alcoholism treatment, a story was told about a man we will call Russ. As a young man Russ went to a country barn dance. As many of us would in his place, he felt terribly self-conscious and anxious. He was convinced that he couldn't dance, no girl would want to dance with him, he didn't belong. Then someone offered him a drink from a bottle. It tasted awful, but he felt the warmth as well as the sting. He had a few more. In a short period he felt like the best dancer at the dance, and knew that every girl would want to dance with him. With alcohol he experienced transformation and had a great night.

What he really experienced was a sense of healing, wholeness, identity, competence, belonging, and freedom. The next day the self-doubt was back there inside of him, because it had never left him. But now he knew the answer. He didn't consciously understand what had happened inside him, but he had experienced it. He knew what it felt like. Nothing and no one had ever made him feel like that. He felt he had experienced healing and found life. Without identifying it as such or knowing what he was involved in, he believed that he had found a way to save his own life, his very being.

Some alcoholics, though I believe fewer in number, first experienced a dulling of emotional pain, a momentary escape from distress. Although alcohol is a depressant, they didn't get depressed; they found relief. Simply put, alcohol worked. It provided a significant healing experience, even if only temporary. This was the case for Beth, in chapter 1, the social drinker who became a problem drinker when her youngest child left home. She had found her *essential* identity, meaning, and belonging primarily in being a mother to her children and being active in her church, which worked only until she no longer had a child at home. The subsequent loss of identity, meaning, value, and of feeling needed brought with it real pain. Alcohol did not bring her an amazing transformative experience, but rather a dulling of the pain and perhaps alcohol-induced *pleasant preoccupation around her motherhood and children.* This was not hedonistic behavior, but rather a way to seek relief and a desire to heal the pain. With a continuation of that kind of drinking, she could be into full-blown alcoholism within two years.

The magical effect that most alcoholics experience may sound overly dramatic to nonalcoholics. But recovering alcoholics will clearly remember the feeling, no matter how many years they have been sober. They will also remember how, as the alcoholism progressed, the ability to get and keep that transforming feeling and perception diminished; and if the alcoholism progressed far enough, how it became impossible to get that effect at all. All they got was sick. Even skid-row alcoholics can still remember that special feeling. However, they are no longer able to fool themselves into thinking, "I will only have a few drinks to get that special feeling." Instead, the skid-row alcoholic seeks a jug to drink to oblivion, which is as close to death as you can get without dying.

## THE QUEST FOR TRANSFORMATIVE EXPERIENCE

The key to understanding alcoholism is understanding the wonder, magic, and strength of that transforming effect. We can see how alcohol is perceived as the answer for brokenness and pain in life. We can see how this can lead into the bondage of addiction—the stereotyped, predictable, repetitive behavior with alcohol that continues in spite of increasingly serious life problems. We can understand why blindness to the problem and denial of it take on the strength that they do. And we can understand why alcoholism becomes a classic paradigm of the truth that if we seek to save our life, we will lose it.

Whatever else alcoholism is or whatever else the causes may be, Alcoholics Anonymous is correct in perceiving it as a spiritual quest in which the alcoholic must "let go and let God" to be free and have life. Letting go and letting God, as we shall see, is the second paradigm about life and salvation that is dramatically expressed in the recovery from alcoholism. If the brokenness, pain, vulnerability, and human limitation in our lives are not being expressed in alcoholism, they are being expressed in some other way. To provide understanding, help, and hope to alcoholics in the congregation and community, we have to identify those behaviors in our own lives.

I had a striking example of this in my own life. One morning I got up at six o'clock to leave the house at seven o'clock to catch an eight o'clock flight to Denver, where I was scheduled for a ten o'clock lecture at a theological conference. Only when the garage door went up did I become aware that I would be driving in very heavy fog. Naturally, I became anxious, knowing that my drive time to O'Hare Airport would be longer than expected. Although my wife, Doris, was still sleeping, I could hear her saying, "John, you need to allow more time to get to the airport."

I had another cause for anxiety. I still didn't have an introduction to my lecture. My drive to the airport provided the introduction. Going south in the heavy fog on a freeway to connect with a tollway that goes to O'Hare, I turned too soon. Immediately, I knew I was going northwest instead of southeast on the tollway and had just added about twenty miles to my trip.

Back on the tollway going southeast, I found that my anxiety about missing the flight increased when the traffic became very heavy. Soon travel was extremely slow because one lane had been closed down for repair. Now my anxiety was very high. I was sure that I would miss the flight. I prayed the Serenity Prayer, which I learned from recovering alcoholics: "God grant me the serenity to accept the things I cannot change, courage to change the things that can be changed, and wisdom to know the difference." Sometimes that helps a lot and sometimes a little. This time it helped a little. I was angry with myself for not allowing more time and for making a wrong turn.

Finally, I got to O'Hare, parked the car, ran as best I could and walked as fast as I could. From the monitor I learned that the flight gate was at the end of a long concourse. Running, I reached the gate just as they were closing the door to the ramp. With a good deal of anxiety and excitement I said to the woman behind the counter, "I have to get on that flight!" She said, "What's your name?" I said, "John Keller." She typed and then typed again. Looking up, she said, "You are not here." I said, "I have to get on that flight!" She typed again and looking up said, "Oh, here you are. You are scheduled for tomorrow." I said, "I have to get on that plane!" She smiled and said, "Don't worry. We will get you on that plane."

Incredibly, I got a seat on the plane. In a short time we were out of the heavy fog and up in the bright blue sky with the sun shining brilliantly. My anxiety had subsided but not disappeared. I then found myself reflecting on my morning's experience and how much it was a reflection of life and our human condition. There is so much fog—the painful, anxiety-ridden stuff in life related to our own brokenness and the brokenness in all of God's creation. Many are born, live, and die in that fog, never seeing the brightness of the sun. Those of us more fortunate also experience that fog, sometimes suddenly and shockingly and sometimes for lengthy periods.

The flight attendant was speaking: "Good morning. Welcome to Continental Airlines. The bar is open." (Airlines don't do that anymore—at least not in my experience.) That made me think, somewhere in Continental Airlines there is someone who understands the human condition. The invitation was, "Wouldn't you like to begin your day with a little anesthesia?" Reflecting on that, I said to myself, "Deep within each of us is a profound, if not recognized, *yes*. If only there were some way to escape from, fix, control, or eliminate the pain, loss, brokenness, limitation, and vulnerability in our own lives alone and together with others. Yes."

## THE STRENGTH OF DENIAL

Our response to our common human condition is paradoxical. On the one hand, we develop powerful denial mechanisms. On the other hand, through our attitudes and behaviors, we make it clear that we think we can escape from the human condition, fix it, control it, even eliminate it in our own lives, in our relationships with one another, God, and even nations with other nations. We also deceive ourselves into believing in our personal human invulnerability.

Denial is not unique to alcoholism. It is a behavior in all our lives. Within the congregation we confess being by nature sinful, but then when our sinfulness gets expressed in our relationships in violations of Christ's law of love, we seek to deny its existence within ourselves by rationalization and projection. It is quite natural for any of us to deny that change needs to take place in our attitudes, feelings, and behaviors. Someone else needs to change. It isn't my problem. When we need help outside ourselves, it is natural to deny it until we just can't deny it anymore.

We may be inclined to say, "Yes, but if my drinking were becoming a problem, I wouldn't deny it. I would quit, or I would do something about it before I became an alcoholic." If we are to identify with alcoholics and their families, who also get into denial together with the alcoholic, we need to identify our own human tendency toward denial. It is particularly valuable if we can identify a denial that finally was destroyed, as happens when alcoholics come to see and accept their powerlessness over alcohol. If we are unable to identify such a denial, than we are really in denial.

I relate here a story out of my own life, which came to a climax after eight years as a pastor. One day I was listening to Dr. Bradley give a lecture to the alcoholic patients at Willmar. He explained that anything that has the capability of changing any negative perceptions and feelings we have within and about ourselves can become addictive. He included not only alcohol, other drugs, and nicotine addiction, but food addiction and work addiction.

While I was listening to that lecture, the light went on in my head, and I could feel the awful pain of self-disillusionment. Immediately, I recalled a Mother's Day dinner four years before. I had preached what I thought was a good Mother's Day sermon about the family being a gift of God. I was hoping, but really didn't let myself know it (denial), that someone would shake my hand and say, "Good sermon, Pastor."

After the service Doris and I were having dinner in our family dining room. At that time we had two young sons. The look on my wife's face was not a pleasant Mother's Day look. It was a painful, distressed look. She gave me no positive comment about the sermon—in fact, she said nothing about the sermon at all.

Just that look. I could remember being upset with her, but not really letting myself know or tell her (denial). *Where was she in church this morning?* I wondered. *Didn't she hear that good sermon on the family being a gift of God?*

And now in that smoked-filled lecture room, sitting among chronic alcoholics to learn about them and their condition, I was suddenly transported back to that scene and my wife's look. I knew now, four years later, what that look meant: "If you really believe what you preached this morning about the family being a gift of God, how come we never see you?"

The pain that came with the sudden crumbling of my denial didn't only have to do with my relationship to my family, but with my eight years in the parish ministry. The first reaction was, "Your ministry has been a sham. You've been telling yourself that you have been doing all this for the Lord's sake (an alcoholic could never use one that good) but it's really been for your own sake, out of your own need to be well thought of and successful and to feel good about yourself." That wasn't the whole story about my ministry, of course, but it was truer than I had realized. Fortunately, with reflection and through God's Spirit, I became aware that God was able to provide some good ministry through me in spite of my self-deception and denial.

My work was doing something for me that was similar to what alcohol was doing for the alcoholic. I now had a personal handle for understanding how our common human condition was finding expression in my life. I could have become a work addict.

Dr. Bradley also mentioned food addiction. At first that reference went by me, but later my denial crumbled a bit more and the new awareness led to more self-delusion. It was less painful by far because it had to do with eating, not my vocation. But it gave me another identification with the alcoholic reality.

In high school and college, I lived with the pain of being on the football squad but never really making it because I was six feet tall and only 131 pounds. In basketball I made the starting five, but I was the skinny one among my team members. I loved sweets—donuts, rolls, cookies, pie, coffee cakes, candy, ice cream. I could eat as much as I wanted and not put on a pound. Those chocolate sundaes with nuts in the evening were a special delight. At about age thirty I asked the doctor how I could gain weight. Even back then, when overweight wasn't a prominent issue, he wondered about me. Anyway, something happened after that. I began to put on weight without letting myself know it (denial), even when buying new, larger suits. Eventually, I went to two hundred pounds.

I finally decided to lose weight, in the same way that an alcoholic decides to quit drinking. I was dumb enough to announce my decision to the world at large, so I knew my family and friends were watching my intake. After a while I began to sneak food, just as alcoholics sneak drinks—but, of course, I wasn't sneaking, I was just having something to eat. I would come home from work and—with a faint sense of discomfort about what I was doing—proceed to make and eat a chocolate sundae with nuts. There was no weight loss. Did I lie when I said I was going to lose weight? Has the alcoholic lied when he or she says, "I am going to quit"? Certainly, that isn't the intention. It has more to do with denial and self-delusion.

Fortunately, I had not yet progressed into food addiction and was able, when the doctor recommended and I was ready, to lose pounds and maintain a desired weight level without outside help. It was clear that food, particularly sweets, had been doing something for me. In the evening, for instance, the ice cream sundae with nuts was just taking a little edge off my anxiety.

So alcoholism becomes a paradigm for identification and getting a handle on the question, "What behavior in my life is providing relief from the brokenness and that foggy, anxiety-creating stuff in the common human condition?" It doesn't necessarily have to be an addiction. *Anything that can change dis-ease in our internal environment can be the expression of and have the potential for addiction. There is no way to know what might work for any given person, or why it does.*

We do know that work addiction is common among pastors and others in the helping professions, as well as among business executives. In work addiction there is the same loss of control over work and bondage to work as with alcohol addiction. But because work is a positive value in our society, the person addicted to work may have a much more difficult time cracking denial and self-delusion than the alcoholic does about alcoholism. We reward work addiction with recognition and encouragement. Think of the perception of the "ideal pastor"—always available for anyone, anytime. A frequent response, even from work-addicted pastors, is that the addiction to work isn't destroying oneself or hurting others, but rather is doing something good and productive.

When we look closely at work addiction, however, we find the same absence of meaningful relationships in marriage and family as we find in alcoholism. We find spouses without a spouse and children without a parent, even though they all live together in the same house. A daughter of a pastor said to her mother, "Maybe if I get sick, I'll have a father." When her mother told this to the father, it went right by him. He couldn't even hear it, because he was blinded and self-deluded in his work addiction.

Robert, a highly regarded pastor, always took his vacations around something involved with work. (Work addicts do that.) One summer he decided to make a change. He and his family would spend two weeks at a lake. His wife Betty returned from the vacation saying, "Never again am I going to put myself and our children through that." The pastor was like a caged animal, always on the move, always doing something. Work addicts on a vacation are like alcoholics on a dry drunk, wanting to drink but not drinking. When he returned to his office to practice his addiction, he was no longer anxious and restless. His spouse, however, was worn out, anxious, and distressed.

As the wife of a work-addicted pastor, Betty had some options. She could get caught up with the recognition Robert received, and which also came to her because of him. Tragically, this sometimes works. Or she could live with the loneliness and anger of hearing about what a wonderful caring pastor her husband was, while not having a caring husband. She could find fulfillment for herself in her own way. Or, as some do, she could decide that his work can have him and get a divorce.

There is a tremendous difference between working hard and being a work addict. In working hard there is freedom to let go of the work, relax, be open to family and responsive to their needs. Work doesn't have the person. The person has the work.

Heart attacks and divorce are common among work addicts. Following a heart attack, when the doctor says, "You have to let up and slow down," the work addict not only denies that needs to be done, but can't do it. When the spouse says, "You are going to have to take more time to be with me and the children," the addict may promise, even do it for a while, as an alcoholic can let go of drinking for a while, but find it impossible to break out of the work addiction. It is unusual for a work addict to recover and learn to live a more holistic life.

Food has always been effective in modifying how many people feel. The prevalence of seriously overweight people who do not have bio-medical problems testifies to that. Some people get hooked and become food addicts. They deny and delude themselves, like alcoholics. They sneak food. Often they eat little in public, leaving friends wondering how they can be so overweight when they eat so little.

A woman told the story of making and eating cookies while the children were at school. When they came home, they wanted some. She told them they couldn't have any until supper. When they went out to play, she sneaked some more cookies and hid herself to eat them. Many of us who do or would like to overeat may not be addicted and involved in similar types of behavior around food; but we can easily identify with overeating and thus with the food and also the alcohol addict.

We are seeing and hearing much more these days about other eating disorders, such as bulimia and anorexia. These also have dynamics similar to alcoholism, including the delusion of powerfulness and denial of powerlessness over the eating disorder.

Success, power, money, material possessions, sex, running, exercise—anything can become the thing that expresses our own efforts to escape from the brokenness in life and the hidden attempt to heal and save our own soul. Jesus says it so well: "Where your treasure is, there will your heart be also" (Matthew 6:21). All of us in the church have a treasure or treasures other than the kingdom that we seek or are hooked on. None of these can eliminate or heal the brokenness, pain, vulnerability, and human limitation. They can be our attempts to escape, to heal, to save ourselves. They can indeed become our idols and even our bondage. But as St. Augustine has said, "Our souls are restless until they rest in God."

Religion can also be an addiction. Unhealthy, legalistic, moralistic, self-righteous religion can become the most effective and deceptive of all expressions to heal and save one's own brokenness, life, and soul. The only people Jesus really lashed out at with feelings and words that leave us in shock were the Pharisees. He said they were whited sepulchers on the outside and dirty on the inside. He said they were sick, but didn't know they needed a physician. They believed that through their religion and religious practices they had healed and saved their own souls. "God, I thank you that I am not like the tax collector," said one Pharisee (Luke 18:11). There was hope for all other sorts and conditions of people, but little if any hope for the Pharisees because of their blindness, self-deception, and denial within their unhealthy religion. Rarely do people recover from such religious addiction.

We have seen many examples of how people can use religion in the name of Jesus Christ as escape from self and manipulation of others. People also find security in the "rightness" of doctrine, which leads one into the comfort and protection of deceptive idolatry.

Anything, including unhealthy religion, can help us identify with the alcoholic by understanding our own attempts to deny, escape from, control, or eliminate the brokenness, pain, vulnerability, and limitation of human existence. At the most profound level, we are recognizing our own efforts to heal ourselves and save our own souls.

Life in the Christian faith has convinced me, as the gospel makes clear, that being born anew involves a painful disillusionment about self that is expressed in the publican's prayer, "Lord, be merciful to me a sinner"(Luke 18:13).

# 4. The Spiritual Recovery Program of Alcoholics Anonymous

Alcoholics Anonymous was cofounded in 1935 by Bill Wilson and Dr. Bob Smith—known in AA as Bill W. and Dr. Bob—two alcoholics who learned that by helping each other they could stay sober. But AA's inspiration came from within the Christian faith community.

## BILL W.'S SPIRITUAL AWAKENING

Bill Wilson had been an alcoholic for many years. His doctor, William Silkworth, finally told Bill that his condition was hopeless and he would have to be locked up. For Bill, this experience led to a terrifying feeling he later described as "deflation at depth"; but it allowed the door to be opened to a spiritual awakening.[1]

Bill's friend Ebby, whom Bill had known as another hopeless drunk, visited Bill in the hospital. To Bill's surprise, Ebby was sober. He shared with Bill that he was living the teachings of the religious Oxford Group, which focused on spiritual renewal through basic Christian principles for living. The Oxford Group had told Ebby that if he wanted to stay sober he had to take four essential steps: (1) admit that he was licked; (2) take stock of himself and confess his defects to another person in confidence; (3) make restitution for the harm done to others; and (4) practice the kind of giving that has no price tag on it, the giving of yourself to somebody. They also told him to pray (which Ebby said Bill would probably gag on) to whatever God he thought there was for the power to carry out these precepts. If Ebby didn't believe in God, he was told to experiment by praying to any God there might be.

Bill noted that Ebby didn't try to pressure or evangelize him, and he could not forget what Ebby had said. "In the kinship of common suffering one alcoholic had been talking to another."[2] Bill drank again, but he couldn't forget Ebby and what he had said about the Oxford Group.

One day Bill attended a Sunday service in Dr. Samuel Shoemaker's mission, the place where Ebby had gone, to see what they had to offer. He was struck by Dr. Shoemaker's utter honesty and tremendous forthrightness. Later on Bill said that it was through Dr. Shoemaker that most of AA's spiritual principles had come.

Inevitably, Bill was hospitalized again, and once again Ebby visited him. Bill finally cried out, "If there is a God, let him show Himself. I am ready to do anything, anything!"[3] From that heartfelt cry came the spiritual awakening and the end to Bill's drinking:

> Suddenly the room lit up with a great white light. I was caught up into an ecstasy which there are no words to describe. It seemed to me, in my mind's eye, that I was on a mountain and that a wind not of air but of spirit was blowing. And then it burst upon me that I was a free man. Slowly the ecstasy subsided. I lay on the bed, but now for a time I was in another world, a new world of consciousness. All about me and through me there was a wonderful feeling of Presence and I thought to myself, "So this is the God of the preacher!" A great peace stole over me and I thought, "No matter how wrong things seem to be, they still are right. Things are all right with God and His world."

> Then little by little I began to be frightened. My modern education crawled back and said to me, "You are hallucinating. You had better get the doctor." Dr. Silkworth asked me a lot of questions. After a while he said, "No, Bill, you are not crazy. There has been some basic psychological or spiritual event here. I've read about these things in books. Sometimes spiritual experiences do release people from alcoholism." Immensely relieved, I fell again to wondering what actually had happened.

> More light on this came the next day. It was Ebby, I think, who brought me a copy of William James's *Varieties of Religious*

*Experience.* It was rather difficult reading for me, but I devoured it from cover to cover. Spiritual experiences, James thought, could have objective reality; almost like gifts from the blue, they could transform people. Some were sudden brilliant illuminations; others came on very gradually. Some flowed out of religious channels; others did not. But nearly all had the great common denominators of pain, suffering, and calamity. Complete hopelessness and deflation at depth were almost required to make the recipient ready. The significance of all this burst upon me. Deflation at depth—yes, that was it. Exactly that happened to me.[4]

Bill also has this to say about that experience:

There I humbly offered myself to God, as I then understood Him, to do with me as He would. I placed myself unreservedly under His care and direction. I admitted for the first time that of myself I was nothing; that without Him I was lost. I ruthlessly faced my sins and became willing to have my new-found Friend take them away, root and branch. I have not had a drink since.[5]

## THE HUMAN ENVIRONMENT OF SPIRITUALITY

Many years later, in 1961, Bill learned of an alcoholic named Roland H., who in 1931 had come under the care of the world-renowned psychiatrist Dr. Carl G. Jung. Dr. Jung had told Roland that he was hopeless as far as medical or psychiatric treatment was concerned. When Roland asked if there was any hope at all, Dr. Jung told him there might be some hope if he could become the subject of a spiritual or religious conversion. Shortly thereafter Roland joined the Oxford groups.

Bill wrote to Dr. Jung, asking if this story was true. Dr. Jung wrote back to Bill, confirming his relationship with Roland and the statement about hopelessness apart from a spiritual experience. He wrote about the caution he had to exercise back then in talking with colleagues about the spiritual, because he was so easily misunderstood. He quoted Psalm 42:1: "As the heart panteth after the water brooks, so panteth my soul after thee, O God."

Bill identified the common factor in his relationship with Dr. Silkworth and Roland's with Dr. Jung as being the "deflation at depth" of having been told their condition was hopeless. This, he felt, was the key that unlocked the door to the spiritual experience.

The early members of Alcoholics Anonymous, out of their utter hopelessness and through their spiritual awakening, understood that alcoholism involved a spiritual condition that required a spiritual remedy. Today more than 1,600,000 alcoholics have come to believe that and are living what eventually became the AA Twelve-Step spiritual program.

Together with the vertical dimension of our relationship to God, there is the horizontal dimension of our relationships to others. The cross serves as a clear symbol of this, and we see it reflected in the Bible. For example, Saul's conversion was not one-dimensional, Saul to God. Prior to his conversion on the road to Damascus, Saul had his encounter with Stephen and was brought into a relationship with an unconditionally forgiving human in response to his anger and intent to murder.

Similarly, Bill's spiritual awakening didn't happen one-dimensionally with God. He had the caring, accepting Dr. Silkworth and a nonjudgmental Ebby to offer him hope in his hopelessness. He also had his visit to the mission, where he met Dr. Shoemaker, a Christ-like pastor in a Christ-like environment. Bill was experiencing through the grace of God what would become a key factor in AA's fellowship: the human environment of spirituality. Perhaps most important and most miraculous, he was aware of its importance.

The founders of AA learned that spiritual recovery happened in relationship with other alcoholics. Alcoholics today speak of going to an AA meeting for the first time and immediately sensing understanding, mutual identification, and acceptance in an atmosphere filled with hope. I remember one who said, "I immediately felt that I was home," which reminded me of the homecoming of the prodigal son.

I experienced the nature and depth of this human environment in a special way when I was invited to speak at one of the international conventions of Alcoholics Anonymous. I met people from North America and South America, from Europe,

England, and Ireland. Even one woman from South Africa attended. She had been sober for a number of years, but had never been with other members of AA. She had received the literature and was living the Twelve Steps. Although alone in South Africa, in spirit she clearly had been a member of the fellowship. When she joined thousands of members and met many of them personally, she was filled with elation. She discovered a mystical dimension in the spiritual fellowship.

During the convention I saw many people meet one another for the first time, and I noticed that as soon as they met, they knew one another. They didn't know one another completely, of course, but they knew one another in a profound way: in their mutual brokenness in relationship to God, self, and others; in their mutual human limitation and vulnerability; in their mutual understanding and unconditional acceptance; in their common experience of suffering, spiritual bankruptcy, hope, healing, and newness of life. They knew one another in their availability and willingness to help without questioning the cost. They experienced and knew the grace of God in their fellowship.

## THE TWELVE STEPS

When the early members of Alcoholics Anonymous met to put in writing the events that had led up to recovery, they wrote the Twelve Steps. In essence they had learned that the natural human behavior of denial and the simultaneous attempts to heal, escape from, eliminate, or control the human brokenness and limitation didn't work. Such attempts led to addiction, which progressively took away their life and brought them to the door of insanity and death. For people controlled by an omnipotent ego that couldn't accept the reality of human powerlessness, there was no room for a Higher Power and there was no hope. They were in a state of absolute powerlessness and spiritual bankruptcy.

The Twelve Steps are the expansion of the four steps initially provided by the Oxford Group. They were written by two groups: the New York group, headed by Bill W., and the Akron, Ohio, group, headed by Dr. Bob. Bill and Dr. Bob met in an interesting way. One day, after his spiritual awakening, Bill found himself in Akron on business. He knew that if he was going to stay sober on this trip he would need the fellowship of another alcoholic. Through a call to the local Episcopal church, he was given the name of a Mrs. Sieberling of the tire company family, who was a nonalcoholic in the Oxford Group, and she gave him the name of Bob Smith. Together the two men founded Alcoholics Anonymous.

The two groups had some differences. The Akron group adopted the four moral absolutes of the Oxford Group—absolute honesty, absolute purity, absolute unselfishness, and absolute love. The New York group separated from these absolutes in mid-1937, because they thought these absolutes, as well as the phrase "get down on your knees" when asking God to remove all their shortcomings were too hard for most alcoholics to swallow.[6] The New York groups also wanted to focus on alcoholics and stay clear of the aggressive evangelism approach and any theological or religious controversy. They believed that there was an authoritarianism in the Oxford Group that was in conflict with the Alcoholics Anonymous principle of "team guidance."[7] Dr. Bob and other Akron members continued with the Oxford Group's absolutes until the Twelve Steps were written in December 1938.

This conflict almost split the two groups as they were writing the Twelve Steps in December 1938. Finally, however, they reached consensus to go with the persuasion of the New York group. They eliminated everything that would smack of moralistic religiosity and perfectionistic absolutes, while continuing to remember and be grateful for all they had received from the Oxford Group. Had they not done that, it is doubtful if AA would have survived. Certainly, it would not have spread and grown as it has. (Many years later, however, some of the "old-timers" who had sobered up with the Akron group still held firmly that the four absolutes of the Oxford Group were the essence of the Alcoholics Anonymous program.) Such a consensus also assured complete separation from any religious group. Bill states that Rev. Sam Shoemaker also modified his belief and position as a member of the Oxford Group so that he was in close alignment personally with the consensus expressed in the Twelve Steps.[8]

Here are the Twelve Steps of Alcoholics Anonymous:

1. We admitted we were powerless over alcohol—that our lives had become unmanageable.

2. Came to believe that a Power greater than ourselves could restore us to sanity.

3. Made a decision to turn our will and our lives over to the care of God as we understood him.

4. Made a searching and fearless moral inventory of ourselves.

5. Admitted to God, to ourselves, and to another human being the exact nature of our wrongs.

6. Were entirely ready to have God remove all these defects of character.

7. Humbly asked him to remove our shortcomings.

8. Made a list of all persons we had harmed and became willing to make amends to them all.

9. Made direct amends to such people whenever possible except when to do so would injure them or others.

10. Continued to take personal inventory and when we were wrong, promptly admitted it.

11. Sought through prayer and meditation to improve our conscious contact with God as we understood him, praying only for knowledge of his will for us and the power to carry that out.

12. Having had a spiritual awakening as a result of these steps, we tried to carry this message to alcoholics, and to practice these principles in all our affairs.

Step One is profound in its insight and simplicity. It has to do with seeing and accepting the reality of their condition, which is powerlessness over alcohol, and a life that has become unmanageable. They identified this as the beginning place for recovery and change. There was no other beginning place.

They had tried beginning at many other places, primarily the place of thinking that they could conquer this by themselves.

Their shame, guilt, and sense of worthlessness had led to swearing off and trying to go on the wagon. It didn't work. They had tried the way of praying to God for help, coupled with promises, while still deceptively believing they weren't really powerless.

The beginning came with their acceptance of powerlessness. This truth as the essential first Step came to them when they reflected back on their common experience. (Such a beginning place initially baffled the professional therapists and is still unrecognized or discounted by many professionals.) These alcoholics didn't have the insights of Dr. Harry Tiebout, psychoanalyst and good friend of AA, on "compliance vs. surrender," which we will explore more fully in a later chapter. The essence of these insights is expressed in the AA slogan, "You've admitted it, but have you really accepted it?"

Step Two was difficult for the founders to formulate. Some of their arguments related to using the name God. The atheists and agnostics in the group insisted that the name God not be included. An Episcopal priest's son wanted the name of Christ. In Step Two they finally settled on "a power greater than ourselves." Bill said that this was the great contribution of the atheists and agnostics. It left the door open for any alcoholic to enter the fellowship and start living the program while being free to understand "a power greater than ourselves" in any way that would have personal meaning and make sense.[9]

Once they had agreed on terminology, there apparently was no problem in using the name God or referring to God in Steps Three, Five, Six, Seven, and Eleven. "A power greater than ourselves" apparently took care of distorted images and painful experiences with the moralistic, judgmental, and condemning images of God associated with religion and also present in themselves. Once those unhealthy images had been set aside, the founders didn't have any difficulty including the name God.

"Came to believe" expresses the view that faith is a process. Some had become agnostics, and some claimed atheism. For most it would seem that their experience with alcoholism had either caused them to doubt the existence of God or to feel that God wouldn't want anything to do with them. They were the worthless in society, the degenerate, the moral weaklings, the unforgiveable.

That phrase "came to believe" is very important. In the AA fellowship no one is told how to believe or what to believe, only that "we came to believe that a power greater than ourselves could restore us to sanity." Members will talk with struggling newcomers about how they came to believe and what their perception of Higher Power was in the beginning. These first members had learned that God was not limited to the what and the how in their coming to believe. There was variety in their personal stories. How any newcomer might come to perceive and believe in a Higher Power was of no concern as long as there was the acceptance of powerlessness over alcohol, an unmanageable life, and the need for help outside oneself. They knew that when they surrendered, a Higher Power was there to help them in their helplessness. Not all, but most who continue in the fellowship come to personally name that power God.

Step Three makes clear that turning "our will and our lives over to the care of God as we understood him" didn't, in their experience, come automatically with believing. Rather, *that decision had to be made.* Within the church it seems that in speaking of faith in Christ as a gift of God's grace by the power of the Holy Spirit, we so often leave the impression that with the confession of that faith there automatically comes the turning of will and life over to God's care, even though there is all kinds of evidence to the contrary. People in AA say something quite different: "We made a decision." That is the behavior of faith.

In Steps Four and Five the searching and fearless moral inventory and the admitting to God, self, and another human being the exact nature of their wrongs marks the vital importance of honesty. The church has much to learn on this subject from the founders of AA. For them it became clear and simple. Dishonest thinking and destructive behaviors had led and will always lead to drinking. It was a luxury they could no longer afford.

The fifth Step, taking a moral inventory, can be difficult but it is ultimately cleansing. When I first began taking fifth Steps with alcoholics, I was struck by the fact that no member of the congregations I had served had ever written a searching and fearless moral inventory and scheduled an appointment to share it with me, their pastor, in confidence. When I saw what a beneficial effect such an inventory could have, I realized what we have missed in the church.

How did the early members of AA come to understand the necessity of the moral inventory and the inclusion of God and another human being in Step Five? It had to be a gift from God. Dr. Paul Tournier has said that we only become fully aware of that about ourselves which we are able to admit to another person. Haven't many of us had the experience of admitting and confessing something to God alone, while still keeping it our "secret"? That, together with other things, assures no real experience of forgiveness or change.

Later on in taking Step Five, I began to experience anxiety. The reason surfaced: not only had no church members done this with me, but I had also never done this with another human being. It became clear to me that one learns only by doing. I think we all need to have someone who knows confidentially the truth about us on the basis of our self-examination. Certainly, that is an essential in therapy. Not all who know me need to know me so fully, but someone does. That someone can become the symbol for sharing my common sinfulness and brokenness with the rest of the human race. There may be times when it is either necessary or good to do this again. General confession and private confession to God clearly serve a basic need in worship and the Christian life, as do confession and sharing in marital and family relationships or with a friend. But, clearly, these are not sufficient.

Alcoholics Anonymous does not think of Step Five as confession in the religious sense. Alcoholics Anonymous is not a religion. The following quote from the AA Big Book about Step Five is significant:

> Notwithstanding the great necessity for discussing ourselves with someone, it may be one is so situated that there is no suitable person available. If that is so, this step may be postponed only, however, if we hold in complete readiness to go through with it at the first opportunity. We say this because we are very anxious that we talk to the right person. It is important that he be able to keep a confidence; that he fully understand and approve what we are driving at; that he will not try

to change our plan. But we must not use this as a mere excuse to postpone.

When we decide who is to hear our story, we waste no time. We pocket our pride and go to it, illuminating every twist of character, every dark cranny of the past. Once we have taken this Step we are delighted. We can look the world in the eye. . . . We begin to feel the nearness of our Creator. We have had certain spiritual beliefs, but now we begin to have a spiritual experience.

Returning home we find a place where we can be quiet for an hour, carefully reviewing what we have done. We thank God from the bottom of our heart that we know Him better. Taking this book down from our shelf we turn to the page which contains the Twelve Steps. Carefully reading the first five proposals we ask if we have omitted anything, for we are building an arch through which we shall walk a free man at last. Is our work solid so far? Are the stones properly in place? Have we skimped on the cement put into the foundation? Have we tried to make mortar without sand?[10]

Before they took Steps Four and Five, they had *spiritual beliefs;* but now they began to have a *spiritual experience.* As I listened to discussions in AA meetings, I realized quite clearly who had and who hadn't taken these steps. Some just said they didn't believe these steps were necessary. Some said they took these steps in the group meetings, which isn't taking these steps as described in the Alcoholics Anonymous literature. Those who had taken these steps could talk about them. Those that hadn't could only talk around them. Many alcoholics have found that they didn't stay sober until they took these two steps.

Steps Six and Seven make clear that they learned *they had to become ready* to have their defects removed before they asked God for help. Inherent in these steps is the understanding that help is needed, especially God's help for spiritual change and growth. AA recognized earlier the vital importance of humility—when humility disappeared, the alcoholic got drunk. Although Step Seven is the only step in which the word "humbly" is included, humility is inherent in all the steps.

In our brokenness and estrangement, we hurt both ourselves and others. Alcoholics hurt those close to them. It's inevitable.

Fred E., a recovering alcoholic, said, "People need to realize that if they are friends of alcoholics they are going to get hurt." They learned in recovery that there is only one way to address and heal that. Steps Eight and Nine also agree with the biblical way. Make a list of people you have harmed and how you have harmed them. Then make direct amends personally, except when to do so would injure them or others.

The alcoholic may need to make amends with a person who seems to be very problematic and even not receptive. Still, the alcoholic needs to fulfill the responsibility and in so doing resolve the problem. Frank, a recovering alcoholic, left someone off the list because of how difficult it would be to make amends. One day he saw this person on the street and became very upset. His friends in AA told Frank that he needed to follow through. With great difficulty he tried to make amends, but was rejected. Some time later, however, the other person restored the relationship. The alcoholic may know or feel that the other person has forgotten all about it, but that is no excuse for not making amends. The alcoholic hasn't forgotten it, and therefore needs to follow through for self as much as for the other.

Even those who regularly confess their sinfulness and brokenness find it difficult to say to the person they have hurt, "I am sorry." Why is that so hard to do? Even if we have learned to say the words, it still isn't easy. Alcoholics learned that they needed to do that without procrastinating. It is the only way to restore relationships. Even more difficult is to make amends with ourselves, to learn to forgive ourselves, trusting in God's forgiveness, to learn to quit beating ourselves over the head, to let go of the regrets, to begin to be good to ourselves. We all need the grace of God to become graceful with our own self.

Steps Ten and Eleven address the ongoing possibility of self-deception, the need to stay honest. We always need to take personal inventory, to admit wrong promptly, and to recognize the need for continuing contact with God and for spiritual growth related to knowledge of God's will and power to carry out that will. This is absolutely critical because of the ever-present subtle ability to deceive oneself. For the alcoholic dishonesty with self or others spells drinking. The word promptly needs to be underscored for importance because rationalization and procrastination can lead to blindness to defects and subtle movement toward drinking again. Continuing on the path of spiritual growth is essential. Not to do so is to allow for the old to begin to replace the new, and that is disaster. Not to do so is to miss the increasing fulfillment that can come in ongoing recovery.

Step Twelve acknowledges that spiritual awakening resulted from taking the previous steps. Again nothing magical. It is all behavior and behavior change. And within that awareness they came to realize the need to share what they had received with other alcoholics for others' good, but also for personally keeping what they had received while practicing these principles in all their affairs. There are those known as "One and Twelve Steppers" who never stay sober. This step is based on all the others. To short-circuit any of the steps is to place oneself at high risk to return to drinking. Newcomers may initially do Twelve-Step work with sponsors or those with longer-term sobriety and only after they are well into the program begin to carry the message by themselves and become sponsors.

Sponsorship is very important. A newcomer is encouraged to select a sponsor—someone who has been living the program well, knows the pitfalls, and can share the wisdom gained in recovery. This is also a key part of giving away to another what has been received to nurture and strengthen one's own sobriety while helping another.

Prayer is included in spirituality within this fellowship. Two prayers are regularly prayed in AA meetings. One is called the Serenity Prayer: "God grant me the serenity to accept the things I cannot change, courage to change the things I can change, and wisdom to know the difference." This prayer contains the wisdom of understanding and accepting human limitation, human responsibility, and human potential by the grace of God. This fellowship of people who have experienced, through the effects of alcohol and other drugs, the chemical illusion of the human delusion of omnipotence and egocentricity, end their meetings with the Lord's Prayer. Fred E. said to me, "John, have you listened to the fellowship pray the Lord's Prayer?" I knew what he meant. The next time I went to an open meeting, and ever since, I have listened to them pray that prayer. They *really* pray that prayer.

The people in this fellowship are keenly aware of their "not-godness," an Ernest Kurtz phrase, and that an egocentric expectation for life is not only unrealistic and harmful but for them is literally death. They have come to believe that while helping one another in their "essential human limitation" and mutual vulnerability, there is a power greater than themselves needed and sufficient for their recovery and growth.

After their initial recovery experience within this program, some become fixated. Their experience only exists for them around their alcoholism and in their relationships with other alcoholics in Alcoholics Anonymous, and does not expand into their other relationships. They do not practice the principles of the Twelve Steps in all their relationships. Clearly, some have psychiatric or psychological impairments that were never adequately identified or effectively treated in the treatment and recovery process. This observation is significant not only for its clinical importance, but also because it makes clear again that there is nothing magical in the Twelve-Step program or way of life. Although spirituality is believed to be key in treatment and for recovery, a holistic philosophy and interdisciplinary team is essential in treatment.

## THE TWELVE TRADITIONS

In addition to the Twelve Steps, AA has evolved "a set of traditional principles by which we live and work together and relate ourselves as a fellowship to the world around us. These principles are called the Twelve Traditions of Alcoholics Anonymous. They represent the distilled experience of our past and we rely on them to carry us in unity through the challenges and dangers which the future may bring."[11] The Twelve Traditions are:

1. Our common welfare should come first; personal recovery depends on AA unity.

2. For our group purpose there is but one ultimate authority—a loving God as he may express himself in our group conscience. Our leaders are but trusted servants; they do not govern.

3. The only requirement for AA membership is a sincere desire to stop drinking.

4. Each group should be autonomous, except in matters affecting other groups or AA as a whole.

5. Each group has but one primary purpose—to carry its message to the alcoholic who still suffers.

6. An AA group ought never endorse, finance, or lend the AA name to any related facility or outside enterprise, lest problems of money, property, and prestige divert us from our primary purpose.

7. Every AA group ought to be fully self-supporting, declining outside contributions.

8. Alcoholics Anonymous should remain forever nonprofessional, but our service centers may employ special workers.

9. AA, as such, ought never to be organized; but we may create service boards or committees directly responsible to those they serve.

10. Alcoholics Anonymous has no opinion on outside issues; hence the AA name ought never be drawn into public controversy.

11. Our public relations policy is based on attraction rather than promotion; we need always maintain personal anonymity at the level of press, radio, and films.

12. Anonymity is the spiritual foundation of all our traditions, ever reminding us to place principles before personalities.

That this fellowship has not only survived but thrived because of these traditions, without any designated, elected, or paid leadership and with individual group autonomy, is truly an amazing story. Given the fact that each member is always only one drink away from another drink, this story is indeed one of the great miracles of God's grace in this century.

# 5. The Emergence of Other Twelve-Step Groups

The initial and continued reaction of professionals within the general health-care community to AA and the Twelve-Step program of recovery was a mix of negation, detachment, aloofness, and biases. Operating on the belief that the drinking was only symptomatic of an underlying disorder, which if effectively treated would alleviate the drinking, these professionals had failed to provide recovery from alcoholism. But not only did these alcoholics in AA come up with a radically different idea as to the primary nature of the problem—the drinking itself and powerlessness over alcohol—they also devised a program of recovery based on twelve spiritual principles. It was quite inconceivable to the treatment professionals that powerlessness over alcohol could be the primary problem, and the spiritual recovery program was beyond their comprehension.

There were some individual exceptions, such as Dr. Silkworth and Dr. Jung. Dr. Harry Tiebout was another. But very few professionals took the people, fellowship, and program seriously enough to be with them individually, join them at their open meetings, read their literature, and listen to them in order to learn from them. It wasn't until 1957—twenty-two years after AA was founded—that the American Medical Association classified alcoholism as a primary disease. The professional treatment community didn't really begin to understand and accept AA until the late 1950s. Today many have crossed this bridge. Unfortunately, a very significant percentage is still on the other side.

One of the other exceptions was to be found in the first major medical, psycho-social scientific thrust that came with the founding of the Yale University Center of Alcohol Studies (now the Rutgers Center of Alcohol Studies) in 1940. Lefty, a nonprofessional recovering alcoholic active in AA, was hired to be on that staff to share the AA experience and program with the scientific and professional health-care community.

At the Summer School of Alcohol Studies, scientists presented lectures on the "scientific facts" to the mixed professional student body, which also included recovering alcoholics active in AA. After a few days of their lectures, Lefty was introduced. He paid tribute to the scientists and their scientific findings and then in his own inimitable fashion said in essence, "Now let me tell you the real story about alcoholism, alcoholics, and recovery." With good, effective humor, he proceeded to tell the story of his drinking days, which were pretty wild. (It was jokingly said that if Lefty hadn't sobered up, he would have destroyed his home state of South Dakota.) Then he told of his recovery within and through the spiritual fellowship and program of AA. These scientists sensed that such an integrated presence and input was not only necessary but desirable within their scientific community.

## THE INITIAL RESISTANCE OF THE CHURCH TO AA

AA was also at first problematic for the church. Again, there were individual exceptions, such as Dr. Sam Shoemaker, Father Edward Dowling, and Dr. Harry Emerson Fosdick. In the early days no people of the Jewish faith were identified as alcoholics, so the problem was within the Christian community.

One problem was that Alcoholics Anonymous was seen as a religion—and a non-Christian religion, at that—because it used the words "Higher Power" and only the word God, not the name Jesus Christ. In addition, most of those who became sober in Alcoholics Anonymous through what they called a spiritual program didn't go to church. For many this meant that although they had been raised in the church, they didn't return to the church in their recovery. Paradoxically, a significant number of those who continued to seek help in their religion continued to drink. Church leaders were also threatened because a nonchurch group was successful with "the drunkards" through a spiritual program. Some of these alcoholics also swore in telling their stories of spiritual recovery. To some in the churches that meant the alcoholics weren't sincere, no matter how much they talked about their recovery being by the grace of God.

Another major problem was the moralistic, judgmental attitude and response that the church, like society in general, had toward alcoholics. Their drinking was seen only as a sin and they were perceived as being among the chief of sinners. Indeed, they were among the moral outcasts. When I began my ministry to alcoholics, I was told that there were two groups of people alcoholics couldn't tolerate. One was police and the other was clergy. This attitude of the church was symbolized in the skid-row mission, where severely intoxicated human beings were preached at moralistically and judgmentally with the message, "You have to repent and give your life to Jesus."

Most churches today have generally come to understand and accept AA as a needed and effective spiritual recovery program. It is understood that AA is not a religion and that the program can enhance Christian faith and life. Pastors or their spouses who are alcoholic are encouraged to get involved in AA. Today alcoholism is seen to exist within the Jewish faith community, and members are encouraged to become affiliated with AA. Many congregations provide meeting space for AA and Al-Anon. Skid-row missions operated by Christian churches or agencies now incorporate AA in their alcoholism programs. Notable in this group is the Salvation Army.

There are, of course, churches in which the only approach is a specific kind of conversion to Christ and they, together with those alcoholics now abstinent in their congregations, can tell of recoveries. They can also tell of how they find continuing sobriety and support within their congregational community. This needs to be recognized and affirmed, even though that approach is not central in this book.

## AN ABUNDANCE OF SELF-HELP GROUPS

One of the most significant chapters in the history of health care and helping people has been the rapid development of AA and other similar Twelve-Step self-help groups based on the understanding of human limitation, belief in a Higher Power, the nature of the AA fellowship, and the spiritual principles in the

Twelve Steps. The first was Al-Anon, for adult family members, and then Alateen. They have an identical kind of fellowship and Twelve-Step program, with no change in any of the terminology. Knowledgeable treatment professionals recommend these groups.

In more recent years similar groups have been established for adult children of alcoholics. A variety of self-help groups use the same kind of fellowship, philosophy, and Twelve Steps: Families Anonymous, Codependents Anonymous, Gamblers Anonymous, Gam-Anon (for family members), Emotions Anonymous, Narcotics Anonymous, Cocaine Anonymous, Overeaters Anonymous, Sexual Addictions Anonymous, and others for addictions and disorders that have within their nature the need to accept human limitation, powerlessness, and help outside oneself.

The Twelve-Step self-help groups offer wisdom and make practical sense, but they are not panaceas. Some people can't benefit from them. Some initially believe they can't and then discover they can. Many need additional help in conjunction with the Twelve-Step group involvement, such as a professional treatment program, psychiatric, psychological, medical, or vocational help. Some discover that their psychiatric or psychological condition was caused by the addictive process and was resolved in recovery within the Twelve-Step group.

Other self-help groups incorporating all or some of the Twelve Steps have been formed to address mental illness, anorexia nervosa, arthritis, amputation or spinal cord injury, brain tumor, heart attack, heart by-pass, parents of a child with heart defects, chronic pain, diabetes, grief, cancer, and other medical problems, including mastectomies, multiple sclerosis, Parkinson's, seizure disorders, stroke, and sudden infant death syndrome.

All Twelve-Step groups are free and voluntary. People who have lived with and found help for these conditions can be helpful to others and can receive benefit from helping others. The basic principles of mutual identification, understanding, acceptance, and support fit well within the context of the religious faith community. AA has certainly provided a springboard for the development of support groups and has made a particular contribution in showing the need for and the way to integrate the spiritual dimension.

It is good for pastors and congregations to be aware of these self-help groups for various conditions within or near the community. The congregation can also be helpful in forming such groups to meet identified needs within the community.

# 6. Alcoholism: Moral Weakness or Disease?

A group of staff at a church office saw a new film that portrayed alcoholism as a disease and showed how congregations can help alcoholics and their families. Some of the staff members felt that the movie was out of date—didn't more recent views hold that alcoholism was not a disease but a moral problem?

The *Christian Century* published an article with the same focus, called "Rethinking Drinking, the Moral Context."[1] The article mistakenly identifies problem drinking—that is, heavy drinking or drinking to escape—with alcoholism. If the article were addressing moral responsibility in regard to problem drinking, there would be no need to refer to it here. However, the article revealed considerable lack of knowledge about alcoholism. Not only did it identify problem drinking as alcoholism, but it made the case that it is a moral problem.

The article made numerous misstatements: medical science regards *heavy drinking* as a disease called alcoholism; *no* leading research authorities accept the classic disease concept; there is *no* evidence that heredity places a person *at greater risk* of becoming a heavy drinker (in the article that means alcoholism) than family environment, character, beliefs, conduct; the disease model of understanding *alcohol abuse* (alcoholism) apparently provides an enlightened, *value-free*, and *morally neutral analysis*.

It is significant that *Christian Century* published an article that attempted to reclaim alcoholism as essentially a moral problem. That a respected religious magazine would publish such an article, apparently without any considered judgment or outside review of the material, is clearly indicative and supportive of a change in mind-set that may take us full circle from moral problem to disease back to moral problem again.

Clearly, the article lacks the awareness that *disease and morality are not mutually exclusive.* Identifying a human condition as disease does not mean abandoning values or excluding morality and moral responsibility. I have never known a recovering alcoholic who came to understand and accept alcoholism as a chronic, progressive, fatal disease who didn't accept moral responsibility for the condition and personal recovery. AA is a moral and morally responsible spiritual program.

This effort to reject the view that alcoholism is a disease and revert back to the old opinion that it is a moral weakness is making an impact on congregations. The issue is still very much alive, more so now than ten years ago.

## THE BENEFITS THAT HAVE COME FROM RECOGNIZING ALCOHOLISM AS A DISEASE

Much good has come as a result of education to show that alcoholism is a disease. In large segments of church and society, people with alcoholism are no longer considered outcasts who are either locked up in jail or sent outside the community to state hospitals. They have been given access to treatment within the mainstream of private general health care. State hospitals have also developed treatment programs for them. Alcoholics in AA didn't label their condition as disease; the medical community did that. But alcoholics and their families have benefited immeasurably.

In 1970, through the initiative of Senator Harold Hughes of Iowa, himself a recovering alcoholic, Congress passed funded legislation to create the National Institute for Alcoholism and Alcohol Abuse. States created commissions or departments to address alcoholism and other drug addictions.

Many church leaders, health-care professionals, businesspeople, and health insurance executives came to believe alcoholism is a chronic, progressive, and eventually fatal disease. Church bodies and corporations have developed policies and procedures assuring that insurance covers treatment. Most states have enacted legislation requiring health insurance companies to include coverage for alcoholism treatment. Family members in large numbers have found access to help and hope. Lives and relationships have been restored with new meaning and fulfillment.

Congregations have opened their doors to provide meeting places for recovering alcoholics and family members. One church body has an international system of alcoholism treatment programs. Recovering pastors, spouses, and other members in congregations are being used as resources to educate and provide help and hope.

Progress has been made in the treatment field, from the initial establishment of inpatient programs to the establishment of a comprehensive-levels-of-services system *similar to those for other chronic diseases.* Such a system includes:

- primary outpatient care

- residential inpatient care for those whose denial, level of motivation, and inability to stay sober require a structured inpatient program to address those and other needs

- specialty inpatient care for those who have serious concurrent medical/psychiatric conditions

- higher levels of service in hospitals for those with critical medical/psychiatric illnesses that also assure continuing focus on the need for alcoholism treatment

- adult and youth residential extended-care facilities for those who need that level of service following their primary inpatient treatment and a variety of continuing-care outpatient services

All of this is to say that alcoholism arrived in the mainstream of health-care services as a treatable chronic disease. Scientific research shows promise for better understanding the causes of alcoholism and developing effective prevention initiatives.

High schools and colleges have developed education, prevention, and support programs for students, faculty, and staff. Youth are receiving treatment and are recovering.

Care and treatment today presents a different picture from the previous history of shame, disgrace, punishment, and death. No longer do you find a frightened, shaking alcoholic in withdrawal sitting in a sweatbox among psychotic patients in a locked unit of a state hospital. No longer are alcoholics who have been "dried out" locked up with psychotic patients in state hospitals, with no treatment for their alcoholism. No longer are alcoholics thrown into jail as "drunks." Skid-row alcoholics are receiving humane care in detoxification centers, many operated by church agencies. In Chicago Monsignor Ignatius McDermott has developed an excellent model for comprehensive levels of service for skid-row alcoholics in a building complex that speaks of human dignity and value.

Protestant clergy are not being summarily and shamefully defrocked; and Catholic priests are no longer being banished to distant places to do rigorous penance in their shame and guilt, with no opportunity for treatment and recovery. Thousands of employed people are not being summarily dismissed with no opportunity to receive help and hope. The wife of a president of the United States can publicly reveal her alcoholism and recovery, providing thousands with the awareness of help and hope.

## RETURN TO BELIEF IN "MORAL WEAKNESS"

Despite these clear benefits of recognizing the disease concept of alcoholism, we seem to be returning to the old belief in "moral weakness" and the old view that alcoholism is simply a symptomatic behavior disorder espoused by some professionals. The signs are both overt and subtle.

Some researchers in medical science are actively producing "findings" to prove that drinking any alcoholic beverage is unhealthy. I don't know if some of these researchers are moralistic in regard to drinking, but let's assume they are not. They certainly are not giving appropriate attention to the long use of alcoholic beverages and the kinds of benefits millions have enjoyed without harmful results to their physical health or longevity. They are wittingly or unwittingly providing material to be mixed into the long-standing prohibition position of the moralistic groups in the Christian community. There is a strong organized effort to get legislation enacted to require potential dangers to be printed on bottle labels and to prohibit advertising.

Other scientists are presenting the case for strong federal action to raise the taxes on alcoholic beverages to reduce the amount of alcohol that is sold and consumed. They believe higher taxes will reduce alcoholism and alcohol problems. That sounds like a reasonable objective that would be acceptable to many drinkers, nondrinkers, and most church groups. However, within this view there is evidence of the old mind-set that believed you could legislate the elimination or control of abuse and alcoholism, even though history has established that as a myopic approach marked with failure. When this proposal is present in the name of scientific and social response to alcohol problems, the prohibitionists within the church community are quick to join them. What a surprise that will be when the scientists meet them at the same intersection. There is much incentive in this for returning to the old "wet-dry" issue—the "sin or sickness" or "moral problem vs. disease" question within the church.

The December 18, 1988, issue of *Readers Digest* carried an article on a speech given by Dr. William Wilbanks, professor of criminal justice at Florida International University, in which he contends that addiction is a myth and that alcoholism and drug dependency are not diseases. He further contends that alcoholics can recover on their own without outside help, including God's, and that the concept of "powerlessness" is antagonistic to the personal belief in self-sufficiency and control that is needed for the "cure."

In a recent Supreme Court case, a behaviorist speaking for the Veterans Administration argued that alcoholism is not a disease.[2] The Veterans Administration was in court to establish that it was not obligated to grant educational benefits to two veterans, because they were alcoholics. Little was presented to the public on the opposition's position. The Supreme Court decided that the Veterans Administration had the right to refuse them this benefit because of their alcoholism. Ironically, the Veterans Administration has treatment programs that treat alcoholism as a disease, and is currently conducting research on alcoholism. Congress, under immediate pressure, quickly moved to pass legislation to prevent similar decisions in the future. However, what the public most likely read in newspapers and heard on radio and television was the position that the Veterans Administration took with the evidence presented by a behaviorist and that the Supreme Court decided alcoholism was not a disease. In fact, the issue before the Supreme Court was not whether alcoholism was a disease or a behavior disorder, and the Supreme Court did not make a decision on that question. However, what was the message from the media about alcoholism and alcoholics? In simple terms it was, "Sin only, not disease," immoral, irresponsible behavior. These two citings are rather dramatic examples of what is becoming increasingly prevalent in our country in the literature and the media.

Some health insurance companies are not simply trying to address controlling the cost of treatment for alcoholics. They are also failing to focus knowledgeably and responsibly on the various levels of needed alcoholism treatment services or the needs of the individual patient on levels provided for patients with other chronic progressive diseases. They are focusing simply on outpatient vs. inpatient care, rather than on the comprehensive levels of services available for all other chronic diseases. Increasingly, they are insisting on outpatient treatment, while arbitrarily reducing coverage related to the different levels of needed inpatient services for many patients. One insurance company made a decision to eliminate coverage for all inpatient treatment as the initial treatment. Many alcoholics need inpatient care as their first treatment because of the nature of their condition and situation. If insurance companies were to make similar decisions for any of the other chronic progressive diseases, even terminal cancer caused by smoking, there would be national outrage. They wouldn't dare do it. Yet they can do it with alcoholism and not cause even a ripple of a response from any sector of society or government.

Why? Because within and underneath this attitude is the old ambivalence related to the "moral problem or disease" or "behavior disorder vs. disease" issue. There is something "different" when alcohol is involved. The message in this development is reaching pastors and the members of the congregation, and affecting their perceptions, beliefs, and feelings about alcoholism and alcoholics.

As companies become more concerned and involved with health-care costs, many are turning to managed-care programs and are letting them limit and reduce coverage for alcoholism in ways they couldn't and wouldn't be allowed to do for other chronic progressive diseases. One major company hired a managed-care corporation for one year with the stipulation that the managed-care corporation's profit and continuing contract would be based on the cost savings. Apart from the individual needs of the employees or family members in the various stages of alcoholism, you can dramatically reduce overall costs in one year by placing most or all of them in primary outpatient programs, whether that level of service fits their need or not. But it is absolutely predictable that many of them won't be able to sustain sobriety in or after primary outpatient treatment and will need inpatient treatment. Over a period of a few years, the overall costs to the company will be higher. Companies couldn't and wouldn't make such a decision on a one-year basis with other chronic diseases. They can and are doing it with alcoholism. More of the same stuff.

A prominent pastor gave a luncheon address at a day-long seminar for pastors that focused on alcoholism as a disease and the spiritual recovery programs of AA and Al-Anon. He moralistically hammered home the idea that alcoholism is nothing more than a sinful and moral problem requiring conversion to Christ. He split the group and disrupted the entire seminar and then left. The issue is still very much alive within the church.

"Moral problem or disease?" "Behavior disorder or disease?" The questions haven't gone away. The attitude of some is, "You got yourself into this. No one forced you to drink or drink like that. Now get yourself out of it." This response has continued to be both overtly and subtly present within society and church. Today, in other forms, different language, and behaviors, it is becoming not only subtly but overtly present in various sectors with renewed focus, energy, and strength. And within this mixture of perceptions, beliefs, statements, policies, and programs, it is not uncommon to see the disease language in the documents, while decisions and behaviors regarding treatment of people with alcoholism don't match their statements that alcoholism is a progressive, chronic disease.

I do not pretend to solve this problem in this book. There is no question in my mind and heart, however, that alcoholism is a progressive, chronic, and eventually fatal disease.

I wish that those people who see alcoholism as simply a sin, a moral problem, or only a behavior disorder would attend Alcoholics Anonymous meetings and spend some time in treatment facilities and with alcoholics in recovery. I am certain that as these people listen to the stories, as they observe the variety of experiences and problems in the various stages of the progression, failure, and death, many would become convinced that alcoholism is a progressive, chronic disease. The clinical evidence is overwhelming. Much of the pressure to return full circle to the old moral weakness view just wouldn't be happening. The tragedy in it all is that the recovery of alcoholics and their families is being jeopardized when they are treated as second-class citizens in the arena of health care.

For some within the church, the moral problem vs. disease issue is easily settled. Alcohol is sinful. Drinking is sinful. Alcoholism is sinful. I have, however, known a number of clergy and laypeople who grew up with that belief who today believe that alcoholism is a disease. I know some who also no longer believe that alcohol and drinking are inherently sinful.

Within the Christian community, however, there is a more fundamental issue. We have a responsibility to find our way through the moral problem vs. disease question to the individuals who have alcoholism and to their families. Christ has commanded us to follow him, and in doing so to love one another as he loves us. All of us ought to believe that Christ concretely presents himself to us in alcoholics and their families, asking us to understand and care. All ought to agree that understanding and care are imperatives in the Christian life.

If an individual or a church denomination within the Christian faith believes that caring means preaching moralistically and self-righteously at alcoholics to repent and believe, that is tragic. The only people with whom Christ did anything like that were the self-righteous who believed they were whole when in fact they were sick and needed a physician. They were blinded to their own human condition and believed that through their belief system and religious behavior they had healed themselves or had been healed in such a way that they were either no longer sinful or were "less sinful" than others. I cannot overstate how shocking it is to hear what Christ actually said to them when he called them whited sepulchers, appearing clean on the outside but rotten to the core on the inside. "Woe unto you!"

Never did he relate to or speak that way with those who were broken, in pain, having shame and guilt, and feeling unaccepted and unacceptable. His response to those who had a different attitude was, "Let him who is without sin among you, throw the first stone" (John 8:7). In God's sight we are all in the same condition. No one is more sinful or less sinful than another. We are met by God in Christ, and we meet one another in our common sinful condition with human limitation and mutual vulnerability. If we are not met by God or do not meet one another within that reality, we never really meet. That is central in the "fellowship of believers." Without that mutual understanding, identification, and acceptance there can be no Christian community or witness. Unconditionally, God in Christ accepts each of us in our essential human condition and commands us to so accept one another. Anything in our beliefs, perceptions, attitudes, and feelings that blocks or inhibits that acceptance is contrary to the way of Christ.

According to the Christian gospel, people who have alcoholism are sinners like all human beings—but no more than others. As we observe Christ in his relationship with sinners—whether Peter, his chosen disciple, or the woman who was adulterous—he is with them in his unconditional love, accepting them as they are and where they are in their lives. In Christ they find new and abundant life. Whether or not that happens, he continues to love them unconditionally and be with them as they are and where they are.

It is unrealistic to expect that the "wet-dry" and "moral problem vs. disease" issues won't remain with us. It is essential that we as pastors address this within our congregations. With education some may modify their positions. Others may come to a mutual agreement to disagree. No matter what we believe about alcoholism as moral problem or disease, Christ calls us to love alcoholics unconditionally. Without that response to alcoholism and to alcoholics and their families, we are not truly following

Christ; we do not have his love and spirit within us. The issue of alcoholism, "moral problem or disease," becomes not only muted but canceled out by Christ for us. His word to us as individuals and as congregations is, "Love one another, even as I have loved you" (John 13:34).

# 7. Shame and Guilt

As Gamma alcoholism progresses feelings of guilt become increasingly intense and pervasive (see Figure 1 in chapter 2). Feelings of shame, although not identified in the Jellinek Chart, are also significant. This is especially true for women, perhaps because alcoholic drinking is still generally considered more shameful for women than men. The presence of shame and guilt can prevent as well as motivate recovery, depending on how they are identified and addressed in the counseling relationship.

Guilt and shame support the idea that the moral issues involved in alcoholism are not excluded by believing in the disease concept. If we are going to provide help and hope for alcoholics, we need to distinguish, identify, and appropriately address the issues of guilt and shame.

## THE DIFFERENCE BETWEEN GUILT AND SHAME

In the early years of alcoholism treatment, professionals in the field became so fixated on the Jellinek Chart that a disservice was done to Dr. Jellinek, who never intended that the chart would include all alcoholism and all symptomatology. This fixation kept professionals from seeing in patients what was not in the chart.

Shame was clearly present in alcoholism together with guilt, yet it was never adequately identified and addressed because only guilt was in the chart. In *Shame and Guilt: Characteristics of the Dependency Cycle*, Ernest Kurtz points out that although shame and guilt are closely related, they are very different.[1]

|  | GUILT | SHAME |
|---|---|---|
| Results from: | a violation | a failure |
|  | a transgression | a falling short |
|  | a fault of *doing* the | a fault of *being* |
|  | exercise of power, of control | the lack of power of control |

Results in:    a feeling of wrongdoing    a feeling of inadequacy
               a sense of wickedness      a sense of worthlessness
               "not good"                 "no good"

## SHAME

Guilt that stems from personal violation of commandments, rules, or family/social mores is different from shame, a sense of failure, of not measuring up as a person. We all experience shame from time to time, but the ordinary experience is quite different from the deep feeling that "I am a shameful person." Many of those who experience such total shame come from a family with a strong shame base. Rigid rules were to be followed, and the family member who violated the rules was shamed and left with the feeling of being a lesser person, the one who didn't and never would measure up, the "not-good" person.

Some alcoholics grow up with this deep sense of being shameful people who never measured up in eyes of their parents. Alcoholism readily feeds into and gives further support to such self-perceptions. Some alcoholics were also regarded as most shameful because of their alcoholism, which deepened their severe feelings of being shameful people. Such deep feelings of shamefulness may precede or result from alcoholism.

Awareness of shame has major implications for pastoral counseling, professional evaluation, treatment planning, and formal intervention. Shame is often very difficult to verbalize, but it is important to learn to talk about shame to receive help. *Shame can be a much more powerful force in denial than guilt*, particularly in women, and therefore needs to be identified, expressed, and dealt with.

Unidentified and unaddressed shame not only strengthens the denial, but also strengthens the need to prove to oneself that "I am not an alcoholic," that "I can lick the drinking by myself."

One woman I know kept her denial intact for a much longer time than anyone would have expected because she had a primary problem with shame that was never addressed. To admit "I am an alcoholic" was, for her, to admit complete failure as a person. Only when her basic feeling of shame was recognized and accepted did she begin to make progress. In my clinical experience with alcoholic patients, I am convinced that some were not recovering because their shame was not identified and addressed.

Another person, Tom, has had an amazing and continuing recovery from alcoholism for many years now, truly by the grace of God. Tom was an absolute treatment failure, yet he was an excellent patient because other patients could benefit from his brightness, insightfulness, command of language, and clarity of expression. After repeated failures in private health-care alcoholism treatment facilities, he lost an excellent high-salaried position, was in and out of state hospitals, suffered a divorce, and ended up on skid row. At one point our clinical psychologist said, "He may be one of those people who has to lose it all before he can make it."

Once he hit skid row he could go no further down. He indeed felt that he was among the most shameful people on earth. Yet never in all of his alcoholism treatment was shame discussed.

Eventually, Tom became sober in AA, left skid row, was again employed, and was reunited with his wife and family. When I asked him one day how he learned to survive on skid row after such a rapid descent, he said, "When life each day gets down to just one singular overwhelming need—'where am I going to get my next drink?'—life becomes very simple."

After I read *Shame and Guilt,* I told Tom that I had a book I wanted to give him. He had been sober for many years. After he had read the book, he was deeply moved. I have wondered what his story of treatment and recovery might have been if shame had been identified and addressed early in the process.

## ACCEPTANCE

Alcoholics Anonymous accepts the feelings of shame and of being a *shameful* person, because all support group members can identify with shame out of their own experience. They are visible examples of people who have found their way to self-respect, self-esteem, and value within their common condition of human limitation.

For *shameful* people, the ones who feel they have been failures either before or because of the alcoholism, the understanding, acceptance, respect, and dignity lived out in AA relationships provide excellent corrections to such self-perceptions. None can be active members of AA groups and *not be people of value and dignity*. There are no leaders. Some have had longer periods of sobriety than others, but they have no special status. Every member is only and always one drink away from another drink. After many years of sobriety one member said, "Whoever of us woke up the earliest this morning has the longest sobriety." Those with longer-term sobriety are needed by the newcomers as symbols of hope, guidance, and learning. But the newcomers are equally needed by those with longer-term sobriety as reminders of what it was like before and in the early days of recovery.

It is necessary to recognize the difference between shame and guilt, although they are almost always together. To be most helpful, it is important to learn how to address the extent and intensity of each. The disease concept of alcoholism, particularly when communicated by a pastor, can initially be very helpful in alleviating the shamefulness. Such sharing enables people to open the door, to take a good look at their alcoholism, and to begin to consider the spiritual values and behaviors essential for recovery. When a person is expressing both shame and guilt by various words and feelings, a pastor may describe the difference between guilt and shame and then ask, "If you had to decide which was more painful for you in your drinking—shame or guilt—which would you pick?" This simple question can be surprisingly helpful in assessing intensity and strength of shame and guilt.

When the pastor and congregation members are emptied of shameful feelings toward alcoholics and their family members, they will communicate feelings of acceptance and will evidence them in education and discussion about alcoholism. Such church communities do not view alcoholics as shameful people. They understand them as people caught up in the predictable destructive patterns of a progressive chronic disease. The disease concept can be used effectively in a congregation to help people begin to let go of their denial that had been reinforced by shame and guilt.

Such an understanding attitude is similar to the relationship of Jesus with shame-filled and guilt-ridden Zacchaeus (Luke 9:1–10), the adulterous woman (John 8:3–10), and the denying Peter (Luke 22:54–62 and John 21:15–19). Understanding, sensitivity, and unconditional acceptance describe pastors and congregations through whom the love of Christ flows to people of all needs and conditions.

# 8. Moralism vs. Morality

From a Christian faith perspective, the disease concept of alcoholism does not negate the moral issues or responsibilities related to alcoholism. The disease concept expresses the *clinically identifiable medical, psychiatric, and psychological progressive aspects* of alcoholism that classify it as a chronic, progressive disease. The disease concept has also been helpful in reducing and often removing the historical moralistic response toward alcoholics in church and society.

When I started my specialized ministry in alcoholism I was told, "You can't be moralistic." At that time I thought I knew what that meant. In spending time with both active and recovering alcoholics, most of whom grew up in the church, I heard what became a predictable theme: that church members were moralistic, judgmental, and condemning toward alcoholics. Ironically, recovering alcoholics reported that before joining AA they had been more moralistically severe with themselves than the church or anyone else.

Though nurtured in the Christian faith, these alcoholics acquired internal belief in a God who was moralistic, judgmental, and condemning. Such a God would surely have nothing to do with them anymore. They had prayed for help, yet kept on drinking. They had promised over and over to quit, only to drink again. They didn't know about loss of control. They thought that if they had any moral fiber at all, they would quit drinking and end what they believed to be their irresponsible, immoral behavior. They concluded that there was no hope for them in God or the church.

When in their despair they entered AA, they not only experienced something quite different, but they heard of a God who was available to help them. In one sense that wasn't new. They had also heard it in the church. What was new was the nonmoralistic, nonjudgmental, noncondemning environment in which they heard it, and the possibility to come to believe in a Higher Power, or a God who was not the great moralistic one.

Having been told, "You can't be moralistic," I was confused when I became aware that the spiritual program of AA was very moral. AA emphasized that the alcoholic is responsible for accepting the condition and doing what needed to be done by practicing essential moral principles. Over time I became aware that my problem, and I believe the problem in the church, was confusing moralism with morality—two quite different attitudes.

Jesus condemned all moralism. He lashed out against moralism. He also made clear that with his coming, in his being, and in his message the moral law—that is morality—was not abrogated. Jesus gave new meaning and new importance to the law of God. He came not to discard, but to fulfill the moral law.

Moralism is not morality. The moralistic life is not the moral life. Moralism is something that permeates and dominates our being. We are by nature in bondage to moralism. Moralism is a human condition for which Christ has come to set us free. Christ is unique in human history as the only person completely emptied of moralism. From the perspective of the Christian faith, Christ is also unique in history as the only person to be the complete embodiment and fulfillment of morality.

## MORALISM IS SHOULDISM

What, then, is moralism and how does it find expression in our lives? Moralism is *conditional* and *judgmental* in love and acceptance, which is to say it is neither love nor acceptance. Moralism attaches strings to acceptance, whether overt or subtle. Moralism is the Pharisee in the temple being self-righteous before God in the presence of the publican. Moralism is believing that some people are more sinful than others. Moralism is seeing oneself as morally righteous and pure. Moralism not only rejects unacceptable behavior, but also the person in whose life the behavior exists. Moralism does this while saying to the person, "God loves you but . . ."

Moralism is "shouldism": "You shouldn't be like that. You shouldn't do that. You shouldn't feel that way. You shouldn't say that." "I" can be substituted for "you" in those statements, because we can also be very moralistic with ourselves. If we are moralistic toward others, we are initially and essentially moralistic with ourselves.

From a clinical point of view, counselors observe that as long as the moralistic shouldism is present in an alcoholic, there will be no change in behavior. Shouldism is nonacceptance of what needs to be changed about oneself. Shouldism is a deceptive way of telling ourselves that we want to change while avoiding change. The alcoholic will keep drinking as long the moralistic response of shouldism remains. Try to think of any necessary and essential behavior change in your life that resulted from shouldism. When you accept yourself the moralistic shouldism goes and behavior change comes, because there is both acceptance of the behavior for which you are responsible and the desire to change.

Moralism needs to have others believe, think, and behave "my way." Moralism needs that for its own comfort and security, but also to sustain its self-delusion and self-justification. Moralism needs scapegoats. Moralism is filled with blaming. We can find many examples of moralism:

- Moralism is the Pharisee's charging Jesus with violations of the Sabbath as he cared for humans in need.

- Moralism is the elder brother, angry at his father for welcoming home the prodigal son by running to him, throwing his arms around him, and staging a banquet to celebrate. The moralistic son who remained at home never really knew his grace-filled father. It is interesting to note how we moralistic humans named the parable "The Prodigal Son" rather than the "Prodigal Son and the Moralistic Brother."

- Moralism is expecting greater reward for being in church work longer or better than another.

- Moralism believes that it knows God's will absolutely in all times, places, and situations. Believing that it knew God's will, human moralism helped cause the death of Jesus.

Moralism lives in the religious box of "do's" and "don'ts," with required belief systems, circumscribed religious experiences, language, and behavior. Moralism is rigid and needs to control; it also fears being free, responsible, and accountable in the world to which Christ has come to set us free. The moralistic box gives us the perception of being safe and secure, while separating the sheep from the goats, the saved from the unsaved. When the moral foundations seem to be or actually are crumbling, there is a great flight into the moralistic religious box, even in the name of Christ.

When self-deluded moralism becomes cloaked in the language of the gospel, it is clearly a gross misperception and can indeed be demonic in the name of Jesus Christ.

History teaches us how deeply moralism is embedded in our being by revealing the great difficulty the Christian church has had in sustaining the grace-filled, unconditional God revealed in Jesus Christ. Think of how quickly the church went from Pentecost to the Dark Ages. Then the light of grace shined brightly again in the Reformation. Think of how quickly the new church segments proceeded to write the conditionalism of moralism into doctrines about the unmerited grace of God in Jesus Christ. The Scriptures declare that faith in a gracious God revealed in Christ is a gift by the power of the Spirit. Moralism can neither perceive nor believe in that kind of God unconditionally.

Moralism not only permeates and is deeply entrenched in us; we also tenaciously seek to hang on to it. It is very difficult for us to grow in the grace of nonmoralism, the grace to be gracefull. Christ keeps calling us out of moralism and continues to promise us that we can be set free from its dominance in our life of faith.

## MORALITY IS SPIRITUALITY

Just as there is no moralism in grace, there is no grace without morality. As Dietrich Bonhoeffer so keenly observed, grace is free but not cheap. Grace is costly. It costs us responsibility and accountability to live out the moral law of God in faith. Clinical professionals are aware that without accepting or being responsible for our own attitudes, feelings, and behaviors, we will experience no change. The blaming, the scapegoating, the rationalizing and alibiing, the self-deception have to be recognized.

Next we need to let go of them and replace them by assuming personal responsibility.

This is the essential difference between the moral principles of AA and the moralistic response of church and society to alcoholics. I have not known a recovering alcoholic who used either the disease concept or the moralistic response as a cop-out. I have known many recovering alcoholics who recovered when they came to accept their powerlessness or bondage to alcohol and then assumed personal responsibility for their condition and the responsibility to live according to moral principles of recovery. A good word for it is "spirituality," which means the absence of moralism and the presence of grace and moral responsibility.

For Christians, morality is Jesus Christ. In his lifetime he lived and expressed the moral law of God. Morality for believers is accepting and confessing the reality and consequences of our sin, brokenness, alienation, self-centeredness, and exaggerated sense of omnipotence. Morality is accepting responsibility and accountability for our personal attitudes, feelings, and behaviors in relationship to God, self, and others. Morality is the behavior of one who believes in the God revealed in Jesus Christ as being grace-full toward us, that is, unconditional in granting forgiveness. Morality is acceptance of the Unconditional.

Morality is accepting and assuming responsibility to change that which is not Christ-like in our faith and behavior and to grow in Christ-likeness. Morality is accepting what can't be changed and doing what needs to be done to change what can be changed, while praying to know the difference. Morality is not only being Christ-like toward our neighbor, but also toward ourselves.

Morality is trusting the promises of God and the sustaining presence and power of the Holy Spirit to make new and to renew. Morality is accepting doubt and even unbelief as still present in a person of faith. Morality is accepting the inability to be perfect while seeking to grow in the more excellent way of love, as expressed by Paul in 1 Corinthians 13.

In any counseling relationship the counselor will be required to make judgments, including moral judgments, about attitudes, feelings, and behaviors. The counselor cannot remain morally neutral and try to be totally objective. To identify moralism as being judgmental and condemning could leave the impression that there should be no such judgment. Not so. Judgment needs to be made as to whether the drinking is alcoholism or some other kind of drinking, whether there is denial, rationalizing, alibiing, lying, procrastination, shame, guilt, and much more. Morality includes judgment.

Judgment that is moralistic *is always harmful and immoral*. When judgment is made within grace, with mutual identification and acceptance of human sin, limitation, and vulnerability, it is emptied of moralism. Such judgment may hurt but it won't harm the person or break the relationship. The truth hurts; but, when accepted and addressed, it can also bring about healing.

I came to realize that the injunction, "You can't be moralistic" does not exclude morality and does include grace. I also learned that the disease concept is not incompatible with grace and morality, nor does the disease concept exclude either of these. Moralism is not within either the disease concept or grace and morality. Whatever the human condition, grace and morality— that is, Jesus Christ—comes to us in that condition and places us next to that person to be grace-full in a morally responsible relationship.

# 9. Compliance vs. Surrender

Compliance vs. surrender is a key concept in understanding what is essential to initiate recovery and why the AA program works. Dr. Harry Tiebout, the psychoanalyst who served on the General Service Board of AA for many years, discovered and developed this concept.

For a number of years, Dr. Tiebout had experienced complete failure in his efforts to help alcoholics. Because he took his patients very seriously, he listened carefully to what they were saying. Many of them said that they were desperately looking for sobriety. Clearly, they were serious. But with all his knowledge and experience as a psychoanalyst, he was not able to help them to sobriety. He decided to stay with these patients, convinced that there had to be something about their condition that he didn't yet understand.

Along the way Dr. Tiebout had become familiar with AA. Years later, in an address to the Twentieth Anniversary Convention of AA, he said that attending open AA meetings had given him hope:

> In that respect my first two or three years of contact with AA were the most exciting in my whole professional life. AA was then in its miracle phase. Everything that happened seemed strange and wonderful. Hopeless drunks were being lifted out of the gutter. Individuals who had sought every known means of help without success were responding to this new approach. To be close to any such group, even by proxy, was electrifying.
>
> In addition, from a professional point of view, a whole new avenue of treatment for problems of alcohol had opened up. Somewhere in the AA experience was the key to sobriety. Here was the first authentic clue after many years of fruitless effort. Perhaps I could learn how AA worked and thus learn something about how people stopped drinking. Yes, I shared in the general excitement of those days. I could see some daylight ahead!"[1]

Dr. Tiebout's experience with these patients made it very clear that whatever else they might need, they needed to hit bottom to quit drinking. He observed that one of his female patients had reached that point. He also observed that some kind of significant change had taken place in her internal environment, a change clinically observable in her attitudes, feelings, and behavior. There was clinical evidence that she had changed from a very closed, resistant, and negative position to an open, reflective, and positive position. She also had something else totally new. She had hope.

Dr. Tiebout had no psychiatric explanation for this change, so he asked the woman to help him understand what happened. Without hesitation she said, "I know what happened. I heard it in church last Sunday. I surrendered." With that she threw him a real curve. Surrender was not in his psychiatric vocabulary, but he knew it was something he needed to understand.

Dr. Tiebout asked this patient to make a list of how she felt before and after what she called surrender. This is what she wrote[2]:

| Before I felt . . . | After I felt . . . |
| --- | --- |
| unstable | at peace |
| tense | safe |
| nervous | composed |
| afraid | relaxed |
| guilty | contented |
| ashamed | thankful |
| pushed | cleansed |
| incapable | sane |
| uncertain | receptive |
| unworthy | prayerful |
| dismayed | |

She added that she had now learned the meaning of humility and meditation. Then she made a very significant statement. She said that she knew she still had problems, that some of the "before" was still present. But now she had acquired new feelings, attitudes, and behaviors listed in the "after" column. The "new" felt good because it was good. And with the "new" she now had hope and a sense that somehow things were going to be all right, even with some of the old still inside. What she described reminds us of Paul's "flesh and spirit." Before, her existence was dominated by what Paul calls "the flesh." Now, through surrender, there was something new, what Paul calls "the spirit."

In trying to understand what she meant by surrender Dr. Tiebout first identified infantile traits he had commonly observed in his alcoholic patients. He focused on three: a sense of omnipotence, low frustration tolerance, and a sense of hurry or the need for immediate satisfaction (my terminology).

He said that "*at the start* of life, the psyche (1) assumes its own omnipotence, (2) cannot accept frustrations, and (3) functions at a tempo allegretto with a good deal of staccato and vivace thrown in." These traits are not described as things learned, but as characteristics of all humans in infancy.

These traits grew into full bloom and together became the dominating, controlling force in their adult life. The phrase "I am at the center and in control on the throne" describes their inner selves. This is called the omnipotent ego and includes a very egocentric self. This is the belief and expectation that everyone and everything ought to be spinning around "me," the self. There is no room for God on the throne and no awareness that the omnipotent ego is an impostor. There is no way the omnipotent ego can entertain, much less brook the idea of powerlessness, human limitation, or "not-godness," to use Ernest Kurtz's phrase.

Tiebout calls it "His Majesty, the baby." The helpless infant is in control on the throne and at the center of the universe with the expectation that "my needs will be met as and when I want them met." Set into the real world, that presents a problematic existence. It is indeed the common human dilemma.

With this comes low tolerance for frustration. There is to be no denial, no delay in having what I want. Think of the two o'clock feeding. A whimper quickly turns into a scream. Any delay is experienced as denial of what "I" need and want. And in that event parents experience who is actually in control: "His Majesty, the baby."

These terms describe not only alcoholic patients, but all people. As we grow into adult years, we don't just naturally grow up, even if we are reared in an emotionally healthy family. "His Majesty, the baby" not only tenaciously hangs in there to maintain dominance, we also tenaciously hold on to control. Unconsciously, and sometimes consciously, we want to believe that we can be in control of everything and we want life to be the way we want it to be in terms of our needs and desires. Saying that out loud as adults sounds childish and ridiculous, but such desire for control is deceitfully, subtly, and powerfully present within us.

In the process called surrender, the infantile psyche is profoundly affected so that it is no longer the dominating force. One who has surrendered is able to see and accept the condition of powerlessness, together with the need to rely on help outside oneself. Certainly, that is a very dramatic change.

Out of his clinical observations, Dr. Tiebout distinguished between compliance and surrender. In *compliance* we say a conscious yes to accepting our powerlessness, but our unconscious still says a powerful no: the picture of a divided self. This state is expressed by the man who said that no one needed to tell him he was an alcoholic—he had admitted that ten years ago. He had made attempts to stay sober, but kept on drinking.

## SURRENDER AND CHANGE

Compliance means that what we know intellectually about ourselves results in no basic change in our self and our behavior. Some years ago it was generally believed that if people gained insight about themselves, they would change. Later it was found that people who have insight do not necessarily change.

*Surrender* is essential for change. When we surrender we say yes both consciously and unconsciously. In the case of alcoholism, surrender is the whole self letting go of the delusion of powerfulness and control, accepting without reservation powerlessness and an unmanageable life. The yes becomes internalized. If the yes is only in the conscious intellect, it isn't present in the person. A Catholic sister said it this way: "The longest distance in the world is from the head to the heart."

Compliance is a conscious event that follows denial. Surrender, on the other hand, is an unconscious process that happens for us and within us. We cannot make it happen. Recovering alcoholics in AA say that their surrender happened by the grace of God. That phrase may have different meanings, but to all it means that something happened that they couldn't and didn't make happen, and it happened in relationship with others, within the fellowship.

Sigmund Freud could not conceive of life without the omnipotent ego, and talked about ego reduction. Dr. Tiebout says that Jesus said, "Whoever loses his life for my sake, he will save it" (Luke 9:24). If one is willing and enabled to let go of that infantile psyche, the omnipotent egocentric self, the impostor on the throne, the old Adam, then there can be life. But as long as one seeks to save that kind of life perception, belief, expectation, life will be lost. Within AA and within the Christian faith there is the belief that surrender happens only by the grace of God.

Dr. Tiebout observed that the omnipotent ego never assumes that it can be, will be, or should be stopped. What a clinical insight! For the alcoholic that means that at any time the omnipotent ego can assert itself and become dominant, with the result that the alcoholic becomes deluded again and thinks, "I can handle it," only to drink again out of control. He said that AA showed great wisdom in focusing on the three aspects:

1. Humility—acceptance of powerlessness, and need for help outside oneself.

2. One day at a time—the way to handle frustration. I may not be able to live with my problems for the rest of my life, but I can do so one day at a time. (I've known alcoholics who had to break a day into hours and even moments in their early sobriety.)

3. Easy does it—as an antidote to the sense of hurry. Slogans, such as "Let go, let God" or "Easy does it," have a sense of humor about self. The Serenity Prayer also has profound value.[3]

Carl Anderson, a pastor colleague, has developed standards to measure feelings, attitudes, and behaviors related to surrender and the before and after. They are identifiable, specific, and concrete. *The focus is not on either/or being present, but rather on what is present when surrender is dominant vs. nonsurrender.* In the alcoholism field surrender and spirituality, or the spiritual way of life found in AA, are similar.[4]

|  | **Nonsurrender Dominant**<br>*Flesh* | **Surrender Dominant**<br>*Spirit* |
|---|---|---|
| Value | Things, money, power, success, sex, etc. | God is ultimate and people primary. |
| Goal | Acquire the above. | Quality of relationships. |
| Commitment | Power, control, do what I want, have it my way. | Faithfulness, integrity, doing God's will. |
| Achievement | Competition, getting. | Caring for others, giving of self, behaving in ways that enhance self-esteem. |
| Self-Worth | Being superior, being perfect, seeking to avoid vulnerability. | Being me, letting others be self, being human, accept limitations, affirm strengths, productivity, responsibility and accountability for attitudes, feelings, and behaviors. |
| Internal | Pride, self-pity, self-preoccupation, insensitivity, seeking praise. | Trust, humility, gratitude, awareness of others, openness, empathy. |

This list does not imply that surrender (spirit) requires rejection of things, money, power, success, sex, competition, and praise. Rather, these do not dominate one's life-style with the belief that to possess is life's real meaning and fulfillment.

Anderson also developed the following listings[5]:

| Nonsurrender Dominant *Flesh* | Surrender Dominant *Spirit* |
|---|---|
| Denial—No/No or compliance, Yes/No (Conscious/Unconscious) | Yes/Yes (Conscious/Unconscious) |
| Mistrust | Trust |
| Anxious, tense | Serenity |
| Hurry, irritability, low frustration tolerance | Let go, let God |
| Dishonesty, self-deception | Honesty |
| Worry about future | Focus on today |
| Sense of being different, unique | Common identification with others |
| Anger, resentment, arrogant, deception, pride, belittling self | Forgiving, humble, self-affirmation |
| Closed | Open to others |
| Do it yourself, manipulation | Open to help |
| Superior/inferior | Equal |
| Keep, selfish, self-seeking | Share, give |
| Self-pity, pride, lack of humor, take self too seriously | Gratitude, humor, sense of humor about oneself |
| Excuses/rationalizations | Responsibility, do what I can |
| Reactive, defensive | Reflective about self—from others and own behavior |
| Doing it all myself | Prayerful |
| Perfectionism | Growth |
| My way | Not my will |

In surrender (spirituality) there is the awareness that full surrender is rare. Surrender is present in variant degrees or with variant strength. However, surrender can be the dominant reality in a person's faith and life-style on a day-by-day basis, and

there can be an ongoing growth in spirituality. But the old omnipotent ego is always there, and on any given day or time it can
assume dominance.

A descriptive listing for spirituality can be expanded within
the faith context to include:

- God as ultimate and people as primary

- Awe, wonder, appreciation, and caring for all of God's creation

- Awe, wonder, and respect for birth, life, suffering, and
  death

- Rest, relaxation, physical, emotional, and spiritual renewal
  with full affirmation and enjoyment of life in this world

- Living for today while having the past meaningfully integrated into the present with anticipation and hope for the
  future

All of the traits listed are observable in one's faith, relationships, and behavior. The presence and dominance of these "gifts
of the spirit" are not possible except through surrender.

When even a small degree of surrender is present in stressful
times, alcoholics will consciously think the thoughts they need to
think and do the things they need to do to keep from taking that
first drink. Recovering alcoholics will telephone their sponsors.
They will go to more AA meetings. They will identify danger
signals through their self-inventory. The compliant alcoholic, on
the other hand, will not consciously think these thoughts and do
these things and will therefore move to denial and the first
drink.

One recovering alcoholic, Jack, told us about a time he lost his
sobriety. Jack always walked the same route to work past a
church. The church was his reminder for morning surrender and
meditation, if he had neglected to surrender and meditate.
Weeks before he began to drink again, he unconsciously started
walking a different route, which did not take him by the church.
If we had known his usual walking route, and had met him on
the different route, we might have asked, "Why aren't you walking your usual route to work?" He would likely have been irri-

tated and replied in a rationalizing and defensive way, as if to say, "It is none of your business." If we then would have said, "Have you wondered if there might be a danger signal here?" he very likely would have dismissed it, but he might possibly have become reflective and avoided taking the first drink. Getting drunk again doesn't just happen. Something has to happen to surrender before the first drink is taken again.

The resurgence of the omnipotent ego is not unique to alcoholics. For years now I have been only minimally frustrated by driving in heavy traffic. One day, however, I experienced considerable frustration driving to work. In my perception it was those other drivers—not me—who were causing the problem. As my frustration increased, so did my anger. A long freight train blocking the first crossing certainly didn't help. And then another at the next crossing. Why was this happening to me?

Sitting there impatiently, getting angrier and angrier, I experienced a sudden insight and began to laugh out loud. I realized that the possibility that someone could have rerouted all those boxcars from railroads all over North America to that crossing so they wouldn't be there when I arrived was utterly ridiculous. What omnipotence! Once the light, the light of God's spirit, goes on in our consciousness, we have the capacity to be reflective again about ourselves.

I began to think about my wife, Doris. Knowing that such dominant resurgence of the omnipotent ego self doesn't happen overnight, but subtly over time, I wondered about what her life had been like recently with me. I also became aware that at work I hadn't been readily available to be with the patients or with the staff. When I returned home that evening, I shared this story with my wife. She just smiled. She knew long before I did that I wasn't in a good place.

The good news in this common experience within the faith is that when there has been surrender and the "new Adam" is again subtly dislodged by the "old Adam," our Lord has promised to be with us in his steadfast love and bring us back. God assures us that the light will in time go on again in our conscious awareness as we live by faith. Repentance and renewal are always possible. That is trustworthy as we live by faith. Thank God for that!

# 10. The Family

The chaos that surrounds alcoholism affects not only the alcoholic, but all of the people in the alcoholic's life. In recent years professionals have realized that many adults who grew up in alcoholic homes—called adult children of alcoholics, or simply adult children—suffer serious personal problems as a result of this early influence. Dr. Vincent Pisani, clinical psychologist, uses the term "family deficit" to describe the kind of situation that exists in an alcoholic home. Most, if not all, members of the family also experience a significant deficit. Therefore, when we think of the family and alcoholism, we need to consider not only the immediate family of the alcoholic, but the extended family as well.

Adult children of alcoholics have identified significant problems in their adulthood and have established a self-help fellowship (Adult Children of Alcoholics, or ACoA) using a Twelve-Step program to assist one another in change and growth. Many treatment facilities have also established special programs for these people. Congregations can assist them to gain access to such help.

There is some evidence that a significant percentage of pastors and people in the helping professions are adult children of alcoholics. For some pastors this can be a primary unidentified factor in their history of difficulty in marital and family relationships as well as in their congregations and with their church councils. Unless such pastors are identified as adult children of alcoholics and referred to the appropriate self-help or treatment program, referrals made for professional counseling may not result in significant change.

The following excerpt from an article written by a pastor describes the needs, problems, and help required for adult children of alcoholics who did not receive effective help in their lives.[1]

Alcoholism was woven throughout the fabric of my family, a fact I could not and did not attempt to deny. But I was in denial over the impact that the progressive family dysfunction had on my own life and my present family.

In 1980, at the age of forty-seven, it hit me in a way that was so terrifying and painful that I had to get help for myself, and I did. It would be another three years before I would hear and understand the words "adult child" and "codependent." Those words, the related literature, the support groups, and the caring people I met who were on the same journey, provided a kind of exorcism for me. It was not sudden nor was it immediately liberating but I learned that what was in me had a name. It could be identified and called out. I could be free from the dysfunctional behaviors of the codependency I learned growing up with addiction.

The family with alcoholism can be a family in which the husband and father, wife and mother, father and mother, child and children, grandfather and grandmother, or any grouping of these has alcoholism. If you are a pastor who was raised in a family with an alcoholic parent and haven't yet sought help, it is important that you at least get an assessment at a treatment facility to see if there would be a recommendation for you to get into a Twelve-Step group and perhaps also a time-limited professional treatment program for adult children.

Because of the prevalence of alcoholism and adult children of alcoholic parents, it is essential for a pastor to inquire as to the possible existence of either of these in any individual, marital, family, or child problem for which his or her help and counsel is sought. If any of these problems do exist, but are not identified for receiving help, any other help needed will not be sufficiently beneficial.

Finally, the congregation also needs to be seen as family for such family members, for all in the congregation are the family of God. The chapter on the congregation will outline ways to be helpful.

## EFFECTS OF ALCOHOLISM ON THE FAMILY

What are the experiences, reactions, and behaviors of families because of alcoholism? The pattern is in some ways similar to that of alcoholism and the alcoholic (see Figure 2).

Alcoholism almost always blocks spiritual and emotional growth for all family members until they receive help. Alcoholism can bring with it the blockage or destruction of any kind of meaningful relationships and communication. As the alcoholism progresses it is accompanied by the threat of economic insecurity and eventual loss of all economic resources, including loss of job, business, professional practice, or farm. The alcoholic may become unemployable. Family members face increasing isolation from friends, social groups, and congregation, either because of their response to the drinking or as a result of the guilt and shame family members feel. The nonalcoholic parent increasingly will have to try to assume the role of both parents. There will be an increase in lonely nights and anxious days, whether the alcoholic is drinking at home or away from home. The alcoholic, under the influence of alcohol, may become sexually involved with another person or sexually dysfunctional. Spouses may live the fear and suspicion that their mates are unfaithful.

Spouses and other family members understandably experience anger that grows into resentment and self-pity. While blaming the alcoholic, they can also become involved in self-blame. They may feel, and even believe, that they are responsible for the drinking. A real sense of failure and an increasing feeling of hopelessness can overtake them. Physical symptoms may develop, such as headaches, stomach disorders, diarrhea, sweaty palms, and hypertension. Clinical signs of depression may become evident. Unknowledgeable physicians who do not understand the impact of alcoholism upon the family will not think to ask a most logical question: "Does anyone in your family have a drinking problem?" Medications may be prescribed that could and do lead to chemical addiction.

Spouses and parents predictably react to the alcoholism with the same behavior as the alcoholic. The first major behavior is denial, the very natural human reaction to problems that cause pain and pose a serious threat. Once the denial is understood at the intellectual and verbal level, an internal denial or lack of acceptance remains. Some outside help is needed to enable the person first to see and then to let go. Knowing is very different from accepting, as the difference between compliance and surrender and the first Step of the Al-Anon program, powerlessness over alcohol, make clear.

Even greater strength may appear in the parental denial of a child's alcoholism. A child's alcoholism includes primary symptomatic behaviors, such as sudden deterioration in school performance, and dramatic behavior changes including explosive hostility, high degree of moodiness and irritability, increased isolation from the family, and a change of friends and even the basic culture of the child's friendship circle. Even when these signals are apparent, parents frequently would still rather believe that the child has a psychiatric problem than consider the possibility of alcoholism or other drug abuse.

Spouses of alcoholics also tend to express behaviors similar to those of the alcoholic simply because they, like the alcoholic, do what we humans naturally do when faced with painful problems that threaten marriages, families, and individuals: they make excuses and rationalize. They blame not only the alcoholic, but also themselves. They begin to wonder about the alcoholic's love for them or their love for the alcoholic. When they do realize that they have a very serious problem, they engage in the natural human behavior of deciding that they can fix it, control it, or eliminate it. They plead, lecture, scold, shame, seek promises, use the "if you love me" tactic, take on a "holier than thou" attitude, develop a martyrlike complex, hide the liquor, destroy the supply, make threats they aren't ready to follow through on, and try other means they think might work.

There may be variant themes, behaviors, and physical symptoms, but something of this is always present and becomes increasingly problematic in a downward progression that inevitably results from "doing what comes naturally."

As early as 1954 Joan Jackson, who had studied the responses and reactions of families of alcoholics, described the kind of adjustment wives (most of the focus then was on male alcoholics) go through as the alcoholism progresses. Although she wrote many years ago, her contribution still has value.[2]

# The Progression
# and Recovery of the Family
# in the Disease of Alcoholism

Blues

Intolerance

Suspicion

Problems Multiplying

Arguments

Distrust                          Worry

Unhappiness                    Irritability

Denial (Fantasy)               Seeks Answers

Threats Made and               Avoiding Reference
Not Carried Through
                               Extravagance
Takes Responsibility
                               Self-Defense
Loss of Interest
                               Depression
Illnesses
                               Irrational Behavior
Putting Up Good Front
                               Self-Neglect
Uses Patent or Prescribed Medication
                               Alibi
Uses Alcohol to Relax
                               Dishonesty
Loss of Self Respect
                               Infidelity
Remorse
                               Isolation
Social Withdrawal
                               Blames Others
Indefinable Fears
                               Escape
More Frequent Use of Drugs/Alcohol
                               Jealousy
Bankruptcy of Alibis

Admits Defeat

Chronic Depression

Suicide Attempts

Without Help

Bottom

Enlightened, Future Bright,
to Higher Levels than
Ever Believed Possible.

Joy                                        At Ease with Life

Courage                                 Happiness

Love                              Return of Respect of
                                 Family and Friends

Makes Amends                          Appreciates Spiritual Values

Peace of Mind                         Return of Confidence

Service                            New Interests Develop

New Friends                         Acceptance

Spiritual Examination              Guilt is Gone

                                   Return of Self-Esteem
Release
                                   Diminishing Fears
Trust, Openness
                              Daily Living Pattern Changes
Honesty                        (Rest, Diet, Sleep)

                              Developing Optimism

With Help                     Begins to Relax

                            Cover Up Ceases

                         Becomes Willing to Change

                       Shares with Others

                      Need to Control Lessens

                     Recognition of Role

                    Recognizes Disease

                   Seeks Help

                  Hope

                 Sincere Desire for Help

                Awareness

The progression and recovery symptoms listed are based on the *most
repeated experiences* of family
members in the disease of alcoholism
or other chemical dependencies. While
every symptom in the chart does not occur in every member of every family, or
in the same sequence, it does portray
an *average* chain reaction. The entire
process may take years or it may occur
in a very short time.

At the time marriage was considered, the drinking of most
of the men was within socially acceptable limits. In a few cases
the men were already alcoholics but managed to hide this from
their fiancées. They drank only moderately or not at all when
on dates, and often avoided friends and relatives who might
expose their excessive drinking. The relatives and friends who
were introduced to the fiancée were those who had hopes that
"marriage would straighten him out," and thus said nothing
about the drinking. In a small number of cases the men spoke
with their fiancées of their alcoholism. The women had no con-
ception of what alcoholism meant, other than that it involved
more than the usual frequency of drinking, and they entered
the marriage with little more preparation than if they had
known nothing about it.

Jackson described seven stages that the family goes through:

Stage 1.  Incidents of excessive drinking begin, and although
          they are sporadic, place strains on the husband-wife
          interaction. In attempts to minimize drinking, prob-
          lems in marital adjustment not related to the drink-
          ing are avoided.

Stage 2.  Social isolation of the family begins as incidents of
          excessive drinking multiply. The increasing isolation
          magnifies the importance of family interactions and
          events. Behavior and thought become drinking cen-
          tered. Husband-wife relationship deteriorates and
          tension rises. The wife begins to feel self-pity and to
          lose her self-confidence as her behavior fails to sta-
          bilize her husband's drinking. There is an attempt
          still to maintain the original family structure, which
          is disrupted anew with each episode of drinking,
          and as a result the children begin to show emotional
          disturbance.

Stage 3.  The family gives up attempts to control the drinking,
          and begins to behave in a manner geared to relieve
          tension rather than achieve long-term ends. The dis-
          turbance of the children becomes more marked.
          There is no longer any attempt to support the alco-

holic in his role as husband and father. The wife begins to worry about her own sanity, and about her inability to make decisions or act to change the situation.

Stage 4. The wife takes control of the family and the husband is seen as a recalcitrant child. Pity and strong protective feelings largely replace the earlier resentment and hostility. The family becomes more stable and organized in a manner to minimize the disruptive behavior of the husband. The self-confidence of the wife begins to be rebuilt.

Stage 5. The wife separates from her husband if she can resolve the problems and conflicts surrounding this action.

Stage 6. The wife and children reorganize as a family without the husband.

Stage 7. The husband achieves sobriety and the family, which had become organized around an alcoholic husband, reorganizes to include a sober father and experiences problems in reinstating him in his former role.

When family members are left to their own reactions and resources, these stages will inevitably result. Pastors and congregations who create an accepting environment and a caring support ministry, however, can make a dramatic difference in this progression. When the spouse and other family members feel free to seek help early, some of these predictable stages can be avoided or interrupted.

## WHAT THE PASTOR CAN DO TO HELP

If a member comes to you, the pastor, because of a spouse's drinking problem, or if someone comes with other problems and you discover the possibility of a drinking problem, you can take several steps. One is to have the person answer the following questionnaire.[3]

1. Do you lose sleep because of someone's drinking?

2. Do many of your thoughts revolve around the drinking situations and problems resulting because of that person's drinking?

3. Do you try to control the drinking by asking for promises to stop drinking?

4. Do you make threats?

5. Do you have increasing negative attitudes toward the person?

6. Do you mark, hide, or empty bottles of liquor or medication?

7. Do you think that everything would be okay if the drinking situation changed?

8. Do you feel alone, rejected, fearful, angry, guilty, exhausted?

9. Are you feeling an increasing dislike of yourself?

10. Do you find your moods fluctuating as a direct result of the drinking?

11. Do you try to deny or conceal the drinking situation?

12. Do you cover for and protect the person?

13. Do you feel responsible and guilty for the drinking behavior?

14. Are you beginning to withdraw, or have you already withdrawn from friends and outside activities?

15. Have you taken over responsibilities that used to be handled by the other person?

16. Are financial problems increasing because of the drinking?

17. Do you find yourself trying to justify your feelings and behavior in reaction to the drinking behavior?

18. Do you have any new physical symptoms, such as headaches, indigestion, nausea, shakiness?

19. Do you feel defeated and quite hopeless?

20. Is your sexual relationship negatively affected by the drinking situation?

21. If there are children in the home, are they showing any stress and behavior changes that could be related to the drinking situation?

Three or more positive responses indicate a drinking problem. You will want to share the results with the spouse.

The second step is to help the spouse understand that his or her feelings and behavior reactions are what we humans naturally experience and do. Reassure the spouse that this natural human behavior is understandable, that he or she is not unique or different. *The reason none of those behaviors have worked is because they can't work.* Counselees need to understand this. They are not failures.

The third step is to help the spouse understand that if the drinking is alcoholism, the spouse cannot be responsible for that. The spouse did not cause it; the spouse can't eliminate it. Deep inside the spouse may feel, "If only I had loved him or her more"; "If only I could love him or her more now"; or "If only I hadn't done this or had done that." Often the spouse feels a profound sense of failure. The disease concept is helpful in helping the spouse understand and come to accept the fact that, "I can't be responsible for the alcoholism."

The fourth step is to make clear the need to take action. The worst thing to do is to do nothing. Refer the spouse to Al-Anon and a good treatment facility for an assessment and recommendations. There will usually be two recommendations: to get into the family program of the facility and to attend Al-Anon meetings. Suggest that the call for an appointment be made right then, and offer to go along if so desired.

The fifth step is to see if the person with the drinking problem might come in to talk about it. The approach to this is described in the chapter on counseling.

Once they are involved in Al-Anon and professional treatment family programs, family members will learn that they need to have the primary focus on themselves and on their own behaviors. This will include the need to learn more about the illness, the need to surrender to their powerlessness over the drinking, and their own need for help. This in turn will include identifying attitudes, feelings, and behaviors for which they are responsible and that need positive change for their own well-being and growth.

They will also learn about their need to detach from the alcoholic and the alcoholism. Detachment does not mean to be isolated from or to abandon the alcoholic. Detachment means to accept that the alcoholism belongs to the alcoholic; that the spouse cannot be responsible for or fix the alcoholism; and to become free to allow the alcoholic to experience and be responsible for all the natural consequences of the drinking. This means no more cover-ups; no more excuses; no more trying to "fix it" for the alcoholic; no more trying to fix, control, or eliminate the drinking; no more getting caught in the denial, rationalization, projection, and blaming by the alcoholic. It means that the spouse and family must allow everything related to and caused by the drinking to just be left with the alcoholic.

Alcoholics either don't want to talk about their negative, harmful behavior, or may not remember it. When the alcoholic is sober, the spouse—at an appropriate time and without an overload of anger—can say something like this: "Do you remember what you did last night? I think it is important for you to know that you did something you just wouldn't do sober. You slapped your daughter and told her to keep her mouth shut. You do have a drinking problem, and there is help available." If the alcoholic reacts with defensiveness, rationalization, blaming, or anger, the spouse needs to let it be. The alcoholic is left to experience and be responsible for the results of the drinking without any moralistic attitudes or feelings being communicated.

The alcoholic also needs to be told clearly and firmly that physical abuse will not be tolerated. If it continues legal advice may be required.

The situation is hopeful when the spouse continues to seek help and is able to focus on his or her own change and growth, while growing in the capability for healthy detachment. This in turn can also improve the chances that the alcoholic will admit the alcoholism and be open to seek help.

If assessment, recommendations for treatment, and an actual formal intervention fail, the spouse will need to present the choice between drinking and separation or divorce. If such action is taken, the spouse needs to assure the alcoholic that it is not done out of resentment and spite, but that it has evolved out of the detachment process. I remember well a group session in which Penny, a woman whose husband had been admitted for treatment angrily said, "I'm done with him. I've had it. I don't want to be involved. I am going to divorce him."

Another member of the group, who had gone for help and had become active in Al-Anon, said, "You know, I finally made a decision to divorce my husband if he didn't get help, but I am sure glad I didn't do it when I felt just the way you feel now. I know that would have been too much for me to live with. I hope you will first get some help for yourself to get through those feelings before you finalize that decision." Penny took the woman's advice and slowed down. Her husband sought help, and their marriage was saved when he realized that he would lose his wife and family because of his drinking. The help she had received for herself first made a significant difference in the way she communicated divorce action to her husband to get his serious attention.

The decision to raise the option of divorce requires counseling with professional staff, pastoral counseling, and talking with fellow Al-Anon members. When such a choice is presented, the spouse needs to be ready to follow through.

If you are counseling a spouse who doesn't follow through on the recommendation to get help or who can't focus on self, but only the alcoholic and the drinking, you very likely are working with a person who has some profound unmet needs and disorder. Such people frequently have a dominating need to be married to a drinking alcoholic, as strange as that may seem. Many of these who divorce an alcoholic frequently marry or become involved with another drinking alcoholic. The pathological need to suffer or dominate or save or to feel needed is still present. For example:

- The alcoholism of Charles, a husband and father, had progressed to the point where he was unable to keep a job. He was verbally and sometimes physically abusive to the family. His wife, Ellen, was active in their congregation, where the family situation was well known. She was considered to be something of a saint because of her patient endurance and efforts to provide for the economic needs of the family. When she was referred for professional help, she was able only to describe the conditions of the drinking and behavior of her husband and the terrible family situation. She refused to seek help for herself. When asked why she chose to keep herself and her children in that situation, her response was, "He needs me."

• Allison made an appointment because of her husband's long history of alcoholism. He finally agreed to get some help and became sober in spite of her. She continued to criticize him when he was sober, just as she had when he was drunk. During his sober period she refused to get any help for herself. Allison began to deteriorate psychologically during her husband's sobriety. Finally, one day she lambasted him unmercifully about an incident that took place twenty years earlier. He started drinking again, and she began to function better.

These are very needy and difficult people to help. In such cases it is necessary to learn and practice detachment, to keep referring the person to professional help that includes a psychiatrist knowledgeable in alcoholism. Typically, the person won't accept help, or will discontinue it within a short period. Such a person may consume much of the pastor's time and create frustration and anger, none of which is helpful to the person or the pastor. If the person does seek professional help and continues to approach the pastor, the pastor will need to consult with the professional.

Sometimes an alcoholic may be in recovery but the spouse may refuse to get involved in the recovery process. This could lead to even greater problems than existed when the alcoholic was drinking. One person will be changing and growing and the other will not, because he or she has operated with the belief that if the drinking stops everything will be all right. Separation and divorce frequently and tragically result after the drinking has ceased. Sometimes the couple discovers that they never did have or could have a marriage, with or without alcoholism. However, every effort needs to be made early for the spouse to participate in a family treatment and Twelve-Step program.

We have noted that parents of children who are alcoholics frequently deny the possibility of alcoholism. They want to see the drinking as symptomatic and to have the problems treated psychiatrically. Every effort needs to be made to help them understand alcoholism and other drug addiction and the need for direct and immediate treatment. Pastors can be helpful in removing shame and a deep sense of parental responsibility for the drug addiction.

Children in families where there is alcoholism need attention. They all suffer hurt, but all don't react to or handle the hurt in the same way. It is understandable and predictable that they will experience some sense of not being loved and a good deal of fear, anger, resentment, self-pity, guilt, embarrassment, shame, and even responsibility for the drinking. There will quite predictably be a deep-seated need to seek acceptance by trying to figure out how to please others, by acting out with other peers to experience their acceptance, or by determining to be successful in school or a vocation, whatever the measure of that may be. The essential reaction and behavior of a child may be any of the following: being the guilty one and the scapegoat; taking on the role of savior or hero; being the mascot by defocusing the family tension with humor; entering into increasing withdrawal from the situation and the family; responding with open anger and disgust and seeking to stay aloof from it all; becoming the failure; or becoming the overachiever.

Clearly, many children will end up with some major deficit. One example is the overachiever who becomes very successful, but has a major problem in establishing meaningful and intimate relationships. This is not uncommon among children of alcoholics who enter the ordained ministry. Although Alateen and Alatots can be helpful, it is unfortunate that not enough professional treatment services exist for these children. It also is not easy to enlist and sustain their ongoing involvement in the help that they need. Having some of this information and knowing of parental alcoholism in a family, pastors can, however, develop some special antennae for tuning in with these themes and behaviors common among the children. It is always wise to seek some professional counsel and to look for helpful resources.

It is important to underscore the need to get a professional assessment to determine whether or not some kind of professional treatment program is indicated together with involvement in a Twelve-Step group. Pastoral encouragement and support of the professional recommendations can make a difference. Through personal research pastors can determine whether the professionals are knowledgeable about alcoholism and if they have high regard for self-help programs based on the Twelve Steps.

There is real value in having available people who are involved in their own recovery and who are willing to talk with other families who are seeking initial help. Pastors often come to know such people in the congregation or community. It is also possible to express interest in meeting some and in asking them to identify themselves. The Support Team Ministry described in chapter 12 will usually have some recovering family members as volunteers.

Treatment services for family members and groups such as Al-Anon focus on what the person needs to do *whether or not the alcoholic seeks help and recovers.* Learning detachment is a big part of that; but it also includes keeping the focus on one's own attitudes, feelings, behaviors, and growth, while recognizing the need for continued support of the group, living the Twelve Steps, and turning one's life over to the care of God day by day.

The need for a formal intervention needs to be discussed with a professional staff person in the family services of an alcoholism treatment facility. At times the decision is for intervention, but it cannot be done because the alcoholic absolutely refuses, although such a refusal is rare. Or the intervention is done without a successful result, which also is rare. In such cases the spouse definitely needs to determine when to present the necessary choice between the drinking and separation or divorce.

When a separation or divorce occurs because of the drinking, any consideration of reunion needs professional assessment, pastoral counseling, and discussion with fellow Al-Anon members. A significant length of sobriety (perhaps a minimum of one year), together with active involvement in AA and the professional recommendations, are vitally important in arriving at a decision regarding reunion.

Finally, whatever referrals may be made for the spouse and other family members, pastors can be helpful in spending time with the children to help them understand. To hear understanding and acceptance of alcoholism from the pastor has special significance and benefit and helps to reinforce what they hear in the professional treatment services and Twelve-Step programs. The way is open for a more meaningful relationship between the pastor and the children.

"God grant me the serenity to accept the things I cannot change, the courage to change the things I can change and the wisdom to know the difference." This Serenity Prayer is as helpful for pastors and family members as it is for the alcoholic.

# 11. Caring Pastors and Other Helpers

Fred, a recovering alcoholic active in Alcoholics Anonymous, said to me, "John, listen to what people say, but then watch their behavior."

Alcoholics often discover that what people say and what they do are two different things. In working with alcoholism we need to be aware that the moralistic stigma is still very much present in society, in the church, and also in alcoholic people and their families.

Fred was raised in a moralistic, judgmental, and condemning church environment. He was physically abused when he failed to do certain things exactly as the priest wanted. The message communicated to him was not simply that he failed to do what the priest wanted, but that he had failed as a human being. He was a "bad person." Such experiences in home or church, or with pastors—who are regarded as reflections and symbols of God—produce not only guilt but a destructive sense of shame.

In his recovery Fred became aware that his deepest resentments during his drinking years were against God, religion, and the church. He was a periodic alcoholic. He had rather lengthy times of no drinking, but once he started, drinking took over all his life and responsibilities. He would just drink until he couldn't drink anymore. In recovery he came to realize that every time he started a drinking episode he had been involved in an argument with someone about God, religion, or the church. His drinking in turn intensified his feeling that he was "a no good person." For him there was no hope in the God, religion, or the church of his childhood.

One day, despondent and hopeless, he stood on a high bridge and realized that he couldn't jump. Later, an alcoholic who had been in prison told him, "Fred, when I was in prison, I didn't drink." In desperation Fred faked a federal crime. But people came to his assistance, he didn't end up in prison, and he kept on drinking.

One day Fred went to an Alcoholics Anonymous meeting. He listened to members talk about a power greater than themselves, and even heard them use the name of God. All the moralistic and judgmental content and images of such language inside Fred caused him to be upset. Yet he was bright enough to realize that these people had what he had been so desperately seeking. They weren't drinking. They were living sober lives. And more than that, they were feeling good about themselves. Strangely, they had also welcomed him. They seemed to understand him and his problem, and they accepted him. He could feel that. He was experiencing that. They didn't say it, they just lived it. This was their behavior. Such love, understanding, and acceptance were part of the fellowship. And they communicated hope to him.

The nature of that fellowship and their sober lives overrode his deep-seated problem with their Higher Power and God talk. The group was indeed a power greater than himself. He returned and kept on returning. And he hasn't had a drink for many years. However, when I first met him, he still had a negative attitude about God, religion, and the church. The look in his eye seemed to communicate serious skepticism.

Over time we became good friends. We even began to have conversations about the Christian religion. One day Fred said, somewhat to my surprise, "John, I want to find my way back into the church." The "want to" in his statement was significant. He didn't say, "I think I should." He didn't say, "I think I may want to." There was no qualification. Knowing Fred, I knew what that meant. He would match his words with behavior. By the grace of God, I didn't give him any directives. Instead I replied, "Fred, if that's what you want, God in his own time and his own way will lead. It will come."

"Listen to what people say, but then watch their behavior." Fred applied that to himself. He began to go where be believed he needed to go if he wanted to find his way back to the church. Father John Cuny, the pastor of the local Catholic parish, was the priest.

One day Fred said to me, "John, I don't know if you are aware of this, but I have been attending Mass here at the hospital lately. Father Cuny, *he's different.*" That was both a tragic and great statement. It said that the alcoholic perceived clergy to be moralistic, judgmental, and condemning, while simultaneously proclaiming God's love in Jesus Christ. Father Cuny was different because he was Christ-like; his behavior matched his words. Fred, in his desire to find his way back, was smart and open enough to recognize that. He was able to determine that his lifelong resentment toward God, religion, and the church did not fit Father Cuny. He was different. This human symbol of God, religion, and the church radiated the spirit and grace of Christ. His attitudes and behavior matched his words.

We continued to have talks about the message of the gospel. Fred was experiencing something new with Father Cuny and continued going to Mass. It felt good. But he was still having difficulty comprehending what was meant by the grace of God revealed in Christ, the idea of a God who loves unconditionally. One day he said, "Every time we get on that subject, you lose me." As the story continued to unfold, it became clear that grace—the idea of God's unconditional love—was just too good to be true for Fred, beyond anything he might think or could imagine.

A retreat was scheduled by a group of recovering alcoholics active in Alcoholics Anonymous who were seeking an increased understanding and integration of their spiritual experience with the Christian faith. Fred decided to go. Here again Fred's behavior matched his words.

The speaker was Rev. Fredric "Fritz" Norstad. Fred knew him, and was impressed with him because of his special interest in alcoholics.

Fritz spoke the gospel message of God's unconditional love revealed in Christ with clarity and eloquence. Coming out of one of the sessions, Fred said, "John, I think I've got it." I said, "You think you've got what?" He said, "In Christ, God is saying he loves Fred!" I said, "That's it." Fred responded with a word he used both in upset and elation, "Jeez!" Fred not only found his way back into the church, but found a new faith in the unconditional grace of God. He not only experienced acceptance with others, but now also with God after a long journey in life and recovery.

Sometime after that I asked Fred if he would be willing to tell his story, including this last part, to a group of pastors with whom I was conducting a seminar. He declined at first, but then he said he would give it a try. At mid-afternoon, after an all-day seminar, Fred shared his story. You could have heard a pin drop.

When his talk was finished, Fred started walking down the center aisle, and I was right behind him. I saw a pastor moving quickly from the side to the center. I became anxious, and for good reason. This pastor unloaded all the old moralistic, judgmental, condemning ideas, discounting Fred's whole story because he had not used the traditional language regarding sin and conversion to Christ. I knew this diatribe would stir up all of Fred's old negative reactions. I prayed a silent prayer. Fred took a deep breath and then he said, "I have only one thing to say to you, Mister, and that is that I am grateful you are not my pastor."

After that Fred was okay. The other pastors expressed their genuine warm acceptance and appreciation for his sharing. I can think of no better story to illustrate the caring attitudes pastors and helpers are called to express.

Are pastors different today? Are they more knowledgeable about alcoholism and more loving toward alcoholics? Education and training have equipped more pastors to be more understanding of alcoholics. However, there is still much of the "old" together with the "new" among clergy. I have already mentioned how a prominent preacher completely split a group of pastors attending a workshop on alcoholism as he moralistically branded alcoholism as "only sin" and the alcoholic as the "sinner" needing conversion to Christ. On the other end of the spectrum, a pastor who may be human and graceful in word and behavior without moralistic religiosity is told, "You don't talk or act like a preacher." That's unfortunate.

For every clergy person or church worker, the initial required behavior is one of personal self-reflection. What kinds of images do you carry around deep inside of you as to what alcoholism is and who is the alcoholic? What kinds of feelings do you have when you think about or face an alcoholic who is still drinking, one who is denying, minimizing, rationalizing, blaming the drinking and the drinking behavior, hurting others and self? If your images and feelings were projected on a screen, what would you see? What would others see?

You can be certain that if those images and feelings are moralistic and judgmental, the alcoholic will see them and know them. I have learned that alcoholics are so expert at being phony that they are equally expert at spotting a phony. They also have the sense to recognize whether a pastor is involved in a nonmoralistic, spiritual way of life related to surrender. If understanding, acceptance, and genuineness are present in the pastor, alcoholics will see and know. The active alcoholic won't expect these attitude and will be confused or surprised.

## BEFORE YOU BEGIN TO WORK WITH ALCOHOLICS

Pastors who are adult children of alcoholics are certain to have images, feelings, and behaviors for which they need help. Adult children who have gained help, including pastors, say, "I never realized that being raised in a family with an alcoholic parent had such a profound impact on me and my relationships with others." Help is available for adult children of alcoholics, including Twelve-Step groups.

If you are an adult child and haven't yet received help, I strongly suggest that such a Twelve-Step group be your first step, and that you call a treatment facility to inquire if they have a program for adult children of alcoholics. If you are an adult child, haven't received any help, and have been counseling with alcoholics, it is imperative that you seek such help.

There are certain things that pastors need to do that won't require great amounts of time. The first step is to read the literature of Alcoholics Anonymous, primarily the Big Book, entitled *Alcoholics Anonymous*, and to go to open AA meetings.[1] This step is imperative for anyone who is serious about alcoholism and alcoholics. Also attend open Al-Anon meetings for family members. When you attend the meetings, remain open and ask questions. Learn to know well at least one or two alcoholics and family members who are recovering, preferably some in your own congregation. Learn from them. Check things out with them. Refer alcoholics to them. Go to enough meetings until you believe you have a good grasp of how they view alcoholism, how they understand their spiritual recovery program, and the nature of their fellowship. Continue to attend open meetings occasionally. Attending Twelve-Step meetings not only advances your learning, but also helps you be more comfortable in your relationship with alcoholics. That good word spreads in the recovery community.

You will also be able to assess whether their spiritual understandings, behaviors, and journeys relate to your own from the perspective of Christian faith. You may feel pain and disillusionment if you discover a gap between the two, but your pain may also lead to spiritual rebirth and renewal.

Pastors will surely be interested in the spiritual fellowship and spiritual program of Twelve-Step groups, not being a religion or a religious fellowship. Members do not worship in their fellowship. They do pray, but they do not engage in salvation. Their only purpose is to promote recovery from alcoholism.

Beyond attending AA and Al-Anon meetings and reading their literature, clergy may find opportunities at area treatment facilities. Staff may invite pastors to sit in on different aspects of the treatment program and to spend some time in discussion with staff. One-week summer schools for alcohol studies on university and college campuses are valuable continuing education experiences. The Rutgers University three-week Summer School of Alcohol Studies includes a section for pastors.

Incorporating sayings such as, "Let go, let God," "Easy does it," "One day at a time," "Turn it over," and the Serenity Prayer into faith and life can enrich and strengthen our own family relationships. Inherent in the recovery is the acceptance of ongoing pain, brokenness, and limitation in life; the importance of going with and through life's realities rather than around them; and the necessity to rely on God's strength, guidance, and goodness, believing everything can work together for good through spiritual growth.

# 12. Equipping the Congregation

How can a pastor help church members grow in an understanding and caring attitude toward alcoholics and their families? A pastor who is silent on alcoholism sends a negative message. Members assume that the pastor has no knowledge, understanding, or interest. They will also believe that the pastor has moralistic attitudes, or believes there is no alcoholism in the congregation. Members need to know that pastors understand, care, and want to help, and that they hope the congregation will be a helping fellowship.

Personal communication in the bulletin, newsletter, study groups, church organizations, and sermons lets members know that the pastor is aware of alcoholism in families of all economic levels, all vocations (including the ministry), and in all age groups, from children to grandparents. What pastors say and how they say it makes people aware of their knowledge, understanding, attitudes, and acceptance of people who are alcoholics.

Pastors can share what they have read or have heard at open Alcoholics Anonymous, Al-Anon, Alateen, and Adult Children of Alcoholics meetings, at seminars on alcoholism, or at local treatment centers. Inviting members to join their pastor in attending open meetings of AA and Al-Anon, followed by discussion, can be very helpful.

Communications need to include the awareness that a person who is wondering or worried about someone else's or their own drinking should seek a professional assessment. Pastors will want to encourage individuals to see them or to approach a Support Team Ministry member (discussed below), a local treatment facility, or a Twelve-Step group.

## SUPPORT TEAM MINISTRY

Support Team Ministry within the congregation is a special program offered by Parkside Medical Services, a church-connected network of alcoholism treatment programs, other treatment programs and social service agencies.

A Support Team Ministry requires the strong endorsement and support of the pastor, but little of the pastor's time. It also requires little money from the congregational budget. The availability and willingness of volunteers to serve in this ministry has been well established.

The primary purposes of the Support Team Ministry are to:

- raise levels of awareness and understanding through education within the congregation and community
- provide understanding, support, and referral suggestions to individuals and families
- identify and establish relationships with quality church-related or other evaluation, intervention, and treatment resources
- explore the possibility of having Alcoholics Anonymous, Al-Anon, and other self-help groups meet on church property, if that is not already done
- provide education on the prevention of alcoholism
- have regular notices and information in the Sunday bulletin and the congregation's newsletter

The staff of the treatment facility provides an initial orientation for pastors. The pastor then announces interest in establishing such a ministry in the congregation, describes the purpose, and asks for volunteers. It is quite predictable that recovering alcoholics and family members will be among the volunteers. Volunteers who have been in recovery for a minimum of one year and are active in a Twelve-Step group are readily accepted.

A congregation may want to join with other churches for periodic meetings to discuss problems, questions, educational needs, ideas, and experiences for mutual support.

After the initial training sessions, volunteers in the Support Team Ministry are installed during a Sunday worship service. Names and telephone numbers are listed in the Sunday bulletin and newsletter.

The initial aim of Support Team Ministry is to educate the congregation about alcoholism. An excellent film, *An Elephant in Your Sanctuary*, helps initiate the formation of Support Team Ministry in the congregation and can be used to educate the congregation.[1]

Support Team Ministry develops plans for ongoing education of adults and youth. It encourages churches to provide space for meetings of AA, Al-Anon, Alateen, ACoA, and others.

Printed and audio materials are selected by Support Team Ministry for display and purchase by the library. Local treatment facilities often have materials for sale. State departments or commissions on alcoholism and drug abuse also may have materials. The presence of a display with identification of Support Team Ministry in the narthex of the church or in the educational unit emphasizes the congregation's awareness, understanding, and concern. Support Team Ministry will continue to inform congregations of materials available.

The following stories will give you an idea of what Support Team Ministry can accomplish:

- Volunteers in training for a Support Team Ministry expressed interest in establishing such a ministry in their congregation, but thought it would be difficult to launch because their pastor was an active alcoholic. Before they had finished their training, an intervention was done (see chapter 14), and the pastor entered treatment.

- In one area where Support Team Ministry has been established, an average of two referrals a week for treatment are made. One was a minister's son.

- During training Nancy, a member of one of the teams, was anxious and fragmented. The treatment staff doing the training and the members of her team were aware of her anxiety. Nancy's daughter had just completed treatment, but Nancy had not participated in the family program. The team encouraged her to seek help. She did, and now enjoys good health and serenity, and is growing through a Twelve-Step program for family members. She is an active member of Support Team Ministry.

- The chief executive officer of a large city hospital, a man who was active in his church, was confronted by family members and peers after they had learned about alcoholism in a church educational program. He reluctantly entered treatment, and received extended aftercare. He is now in recovery and has gained back his self-respect and the admiration of those who were involved.

Support Team Ministry can do much toward making the church a place of welcome for recovering alcoholics and families of alcoholics. One congregation published this notice, entitled, "A Welcoming Word":

To all AA, Al-Anon, and ACoA members, welcome home! No longer will you have to feel it is necessary to travel downtown, to another suburb, or even to another parish to attend meetings and have your own needs met.

Your MEND Ministry Outreach Team wishes to announce and invite you to attend AA, Al-Anon, or ACoA meetings right here in our own Parish Ministry Center every Wednesday evening at 8:00 P.M. Recognizing that alcohol/substance abuse is an illness, we hope that you will feel free to share your journey within our parish family in an atmosphere of strict confidentiality and respect. There is no place like home!

For those of you out there who are confused and wondering what this is all about, Alcoholics Anonymous (for the recovering alcoholic), Al-Anon (for family members), and ACoA (for adult children who grew up in homes where there was an alcoholic parent) are all nonprofessional self-help fellowships that are vital resources which aid in recovery, help provide significant insight into the illness itself, and offer real signs of hope. Peace comes from understanding. New members are ALWAYS welcome.

Support Team Ministry is currently the best way to equip a congregation to help alcoholics and their family members and to assure ongoing education.

The next phase in the Support Team Ministry is a focus on prevention. The booklet *Chemical Health* is an excellent resource for Support Team Ministry. It addresses healthy use and nonuse

high-risk family situations, response to alcoholism, and prevention.[2]

## "DOES THE PASTOR DRINK?"

One question frequently arises: "Do the pastor and his or her
spouse drink or not drink?" In a sense this is an individual matter and ought not be of any concern to members of the congregation. In your congregation it may not be a significant moral
question. Or it may still be true that in some congregations
drinking is considered permissible for members but not for the
pastor and spouse. It could be that your denomination has a
total abstinence position. However, I have known pastors and
spouses in such denominations who did use alcohol without the
knowledge of their congregations.

How and if the pastor and congregation address this question
in the congregation probably has to be left to the discretion of the
pastor. But the question will be there in many congregations,
and in many the pastor and his or her spouse may be accepted
as social drinkers.

It is very important for the pastor to clearly communicate acceptance of people who do and don't drink, and of alcoholics
who are still drinking as well as those in recovery. Any trace of
moralism or conditionalness with regard to any drinking will be
evident and problematic for alcoholics and their family members.
Apart from that, alcoholics and family members in recovery generally have no concerns whether pastor and spouse drink or ab-
stain.

In addressing alcoholism and other drug addictions, congregation and pastor have an opportunity to give expression to spirituality in Christian community, a gathering of caring people
who are helping others within and outside the congregation.

The following story of a pastor's ministry expresses this beau-
tifully:

In the first phase of his ministry the pastor saw the people in
the river and himself standing on the bank, telling them how to
climb up on the bank where he was. In the second phase of his
ministry, he saw himself on the bank of the river helping the
people climb up on the bank where he was. In the third phase

of his ministry, he had gained wisdom and understanding: He was in the river with the people. They were holding up one another and underneath them all were the everlasting arms of God.

Alcoholics and their families, and all members of the congregation, need people—pastors and members—who hold up one another, supported by the abundant grace of God in Jesus Christ.

# 13. Counseling Alcoholics and Family Members

Pastors are called on for many kinds of counseling. Because of this, clergy will want to establish a concerned helpful relationship with alcoholics and their families, and refer them as soon as possible to professional services, to Alcoholics Anonymous, and to other Twelve-Step groups. After they have entered treatment and support groups, pastors need to continue to show interest and concern.

Years of research and experience underscore the importance of arranging for alcoholics or family members to go for help whether or not they want to go. Although legal commitment is not possible today, it is very important to get alcoholics into treatment, no matter how resistant they are. Forty years ago alcoholics who were legally committed to a state hospital were found to do just as well in treatment and recovery as the voluntary patients. The key was the detoxification and restoration of the thinking processes, which made it possible to make contact with patients and enabled them to learn about alcoholism and to hear and relate to the stories of recovering alcoholics. In the absence of legal commitment, family members and employers who understand and accept alcoholism, together with the pastor, can frequently exert pressure to go for an assessment, or if indicated, to make an intervention to enter treatment.

Pastors can help inform families about employee assistance programs. In some plans the spouse may have access to the program without jeopardizing the alcoholic's job. Many companies send the information on the program to the home so spouses can be familiar with it. If there is evidence of impairment in job performance, the employee assistance programs can often provide the best opportunity to help the alcoholic go for treatment. When none of this works, a formal intervention (see chapter 14) can be planned and scheduled.

If the spouse or significant other is reluctant or refuses to seek help, a pastor may need to be firm. If there is continuing refusal, pastors can say that they are not willing to continue to meet further unless the spouse is willing to attend Al-Anon meetings or seek a professional assessment and to follow through on the recommendations. Family members need help for themselves, whether the alcoholic ever goes for help or not.

## COUNSELING THE ALCOHOLIC

As a counseling pastor, listen to the spouse describe and ventilate feelings regarding the drinking and disruptive behavior. Then ask, "Does your spouse know that you are here talking about the drinking?" The answer may be, "Yes, but I couldn't get my wife to come along." Or it may be, "No, if my husband knew I was here talking about the drinking, I would really be in trouble."

It is important to help the person realize and accept the need to be open and honest in telling his or her alcoholic spouse. If there is an angry response, the person needs to let it be and not react. The significant message in this is that the alcoholic at least hears that the spouse is concerned to the point of seeking help.

To the first response, "Yes, but I couldn't get my wife to come," your response can be, "I would like you to tell your wife, when sober, that I said *I would like to see how she feels about the drinking.*" To the second response, "No, if my husband knew I was here talking about the drinking, I would really be in trouble," your response can be, "It is important for him to know that you have been to see me and that I said *I would like to know how he feels about the drinking.*"

Each of these responses is a way of staying close to the alcoholic's ego. The alcoholic has been hearing from others *how they feel about his or her drinking.* You could well be the first, and perhaps for the alcoholic the most unlikely person, to express an interest in *how he or she feels about it.*

There is a good chance that the alcoholic, or the person with the perceived drinking problem, will then agree to come and see you. If not, you could phone or visit the person when he or she is sober to share your interest and concern. If the person refuses to see you, you have taken a significant initiative in establishing a future relationship. The important thing is that you communicate no moralistic or judgmental feelings.

If the person with the drinking problem reacts angrily toward the spouse and refuses to see the pastor, it is important for the spouse to say, "I want you to know that I am going to continue to seek help for myself." If the problem drinker agrees to meet with the pastor, the spouse needs to say, "The pastor said that it would be good, *if it is okay with you,* that I come with you." Usually, that works. If the response is negative, then let the person come alone. The important thing is that the alcoholic is willing to see you.

When the person comes to see you or you go to see the person, remember the symptoms of alcoholism: denial, projection, rationalization, alibis, minimizing the drinking, excuses, and aggressive or passive anger. They go with alcoholism as a temperature goes with an infection. Expect any or all of them. Accept them without being personally threatened or defensive. Just let them be.

You want the person to know you are listening and taking him or her seriously. You also want to stay out in front of the person's alcoholic denying, projecting, defensive maneuverings, and manipulations and do your best to keep the focus on the drinking, rather than on those other things. This is something the alcoholic doesn't expect and hasn't yet experienced. This means that in your relationship regarding his or her drinking, the usual and predictable reactions don't occur. You're not playing the game the alcoholic typically, automatically plays. That game the alcoholic always wins. This is new. It catches him or her inwardly off guard.

You might begin by saying, "As you know, your wife came to see me because she was concerned about and upset over your drinking. I am glad you agreed to come and see me. I am really interested in knowing *how you see your drinking and how you feel about it.*"

Listen carefully and ask questions, but don't be threatened by the reactions and behaviors described above. Don't focus on them. Don't react defensively to them. Just let them be. Don't argue with the alcoholic. You want the person to know you are listening.

Some typical reactions include the following:

- "I don't have a drinking problem."
- "If you really knew my wife/husband . . ."
- "If it isn't my drinking it's something else."
- "Oh, he's/she's always complaining about something."
- "If you knew the problems I have at work . . ."
- "I can take it or leave it."

Unless the person has a character disorder, which means no conscious feeling of guilt or shame, you will hear expressions that indicate something about the drinking is indeed bothering the alcoholic. Or something may be said that will enable you to keep the focus where it needs to be, on the drinking.

You might get a hint that the drinking is bothering the person:

- "I know I drink too much sometimes."
- "I did overdo it last Friday night at the party."
- "I know I drink too much sometimes, but I can take it or leave it."

No matter what else is said about anyone, or about the drinking, together with such statements, your response needs to be addressed to the statements above. For example, if the person says,"I know I drink too much sometimes," you can begin, "You said that you know you drink too much sometimes. What do you mean by that?" After listening to the answer, ask, "How does that happen? Do you just decide sometimes that you are going to drink too much and get drunk?" In this way you stay close to the ego within and keep the focus on the drinking at the same time.

You may be surprised to hear within the response something like this: "No, I just don't decide or plan to drink too much. You know how it goes. You are with the group after work. You get to drinking and talking." Or, "You go to a party, start celebrating, and you just end up drinking too much." Or, "I don't plan it. I'm just going to have a drink before getting dinner ready and before my husband comes home, but it gets away from me." Or, "I go to a cocktail party, and I get carried away."

You respond, "So you don't plan or decide you are going to drink that much? You know, as I listen to you, I hear you say you really don't intend to drink that much *sometimes*, but it just happens. Is that right?

"That makes me wonder whether or not you may be experiencing loss of control *over some of your drinking*." (The spouse may have described this happening more often, but you are staying with what the alcoholic is saying.)

The reply may be, "No, that's not the problem. I can take it or leave it." Or, "What do you mean by that?"

You say, "I'm not talking about taking or leaving it. Loss of control is different from being able to take it or leave it. Loss of control is the inability to drink within and according to your own intention, the inability to control how much you drink."

"I don't drink too much every time I drink."

"It doesn't have to be every time. But once a person's drinking crosses into loss of control, there will be a progressive loss of control over more of the drinking and eventually all of the drinking. We don't know why some people lose control over their drinking. Some have it from the time of their first drink. That may be genetic. Others have a number of years of controlled drinking, may drink too much occasionally or frequently, but then develop loss of control. They end up drinking more than they intend to with increasing frequency at inappropriate times and occasions. They don't intend to drink like that. They are only going to have a couple or a few or get a little high and they keep right on drinking. And they keep doing that even though it causes increasing problems for themselves and others. About one out of ten or twelve who drink develops loss of control.

"I am wondering—and you need to wonder—if you are experiencing loss of control in *some of your drinking*. Have you ever tried to keep from drinking too much over against taking it or leaving it?"

"How do you mean?"

"There is an easy way to find out if you have loss of control. It is called the 'acid test.' You decide what would be a reasonable number of drinks for any twenty-four hour period and then see if you can stay within that limit for a period of three months. If you were to try that, what do you think would be reasonable? A drink is one beer, six ounces of wine, or one-and-one-half ounces of hard liquor. How many in a twenty-four hour period?"

You seek to have the person set a limit of no more than three drinks in a twenty-four-hour period. Now you are "inside" the alcoholic. The alcoholic wants to keep drinking and believes that such control within set limits is possible. You are also setting the stage for the alcoholism to prove itself to the person who has it, while communicating a nonmoralistic attitude about the drinking.

The person may say, "Two, three, four." One man who was a binge drinker actually said, "Twenty." I said, "Wow, that's an awful lot of booze." He replied, "You don't know how I drink." We talked about a lesser amount. The following week he called from out of state and said, "It wouldn't have made any difference if I had said fifty. How do I get into treatment?"

Another man was confident he could pass the acid test. When he failed he wanted to try it again because he felt that he just hadn't tried hard enough. When he failed a second time he agreed to enter treatment.

Try to work out something that is reasonable. That you, the pastor, are setting the stage for the alcoholic to continue to drink is both a surprise and good news, because the person isn't ready to think about quitting yet. If you are not comfortable in discussing the acid test, then a referral for professional assessment can be made.

If the drinking is obviously severely out of control, you may make the statement, "Given the nature of your drinking, it is so clear to me that you need a professional assessment that I wouldn't suggest this test at all for you. If you were able to control your drinking, you would have done so by now, given the way it has hurt you and others. But if you are not ready to accept that and go for assessment, you can still try this test. You will find, however, that you won't make it. When loss of control is so evident, I don't see any possibility of you drinking with control for three months. You really need to get a professional assessment and that is what I am recommending."

If, however, it is your judgment that the acid test would be appropriate and of value, you are letting the person know that loss of control is alcoholism. You also need to share that if the person has alcoholism, outside help is going to be needed or the alcoholism will only get progressively worse. If it is alcoholism, the sooner treatment, the better.

The alcoholic expected to avoid the subject of drinking and to talk about the spouse, job, kids, or whatever. In the past he or she has always been able to manipulate that. This time, however, the focus has been on the drinking because that is where you have kept it.

Once the alcoholic has heard the phrase "loss of control" versus the ability "to take it or leave it," the drinking will never be the same again. The drinking has been spoiled. Whenever there is "loss of control" drinking, from then on both you and that phrase will be present in the alcoholic. It is quite amazing how once a denying alcoholic has heard that phrase, he or she can never dismiss it completely. It lurks within, raising the question again and again, "Could it be that you have loss of control?"

A very angry, pompous, denying alcoholic came to see me following his wife's visit. She had told her husband that I wanted to see him and hear how he felt about his drinking. She didn't think he would come, but he did. It was quickly clear that this would be a short session. He said he didn't have a drinking problem. It was none of my business. And if he did have a problem, he would handle it. My response was, "You will unless you have loss of control over your drinking." That stopped him short. He wanted to know what I meant by that. I described the acid test. He said he could control his drinking. He didn't have a problem.

At that time—so he thought—he was able to complete his work in the morning and then go to the bar at noon. It was nobody's business but his own. His wife had a beautiful home, car, furs, and all the rest. She had nothing to complain about. I knew that when he went to the bar, possibly saying, "I'll show him," I would be figuratively at his side and he would remember the phrase "loss of control."

He was able to control his drinking for the next few days, but by the weekend he was at the bar drinking late into the evening.

With him the next morning was the question: "Loss of control?" He never did come to see me again, but his drinking was spoiled, which is an important step along the way to surrender.

Once someone has indicated interest in trying the acid test, it is important to state that the person doesn't have to drink or drink the limit each day. In fact, it is better to see if there can be some flexibility in not drinking every day and in varying the amounts within the total daily limit—knowing, however, that the person is free to drink the full amount every day if so desired. Two key dynamics in this kind of sharing is your obvious freedom and flexibility to let the person carry out this experiment. You also need to make it clear that there can be no exceptions on any day within the three months for any reason such as birthdays, anniversaries, retirements, weddings, or holidays.

If the person decides to do this, then talk about driving. "Do you drive when you drink too much?" If the answer is yes, then say, "It is important that you don't drive if you have more than two drinks within two hours while on this test. Call a cab. Call your spouse. Don't get behind the wheel. You have heard of drunk driving accidents and deaths. You may or may not be aware that a high percentage of hit-and-run accidents are caused by alcoholics who were in a blackout—having memory loss for short or long periods of time. The law will hold you accountable for any accident, injury, or death if you are driving under the influence, whether you remember it or not."

There needs to be an understanding among you, the person, and spouse that if the one with the drinking problem is unable to stay within the set daily limit, one of them will call. You will want to try to build into the agreement that if the person is unable to stay within the limit, a professional evaluation will be scheduled.

You have indeed been "with the alcoholic" or the person who may have a drinking problem during this conversation and have stayed close to his or her ego. You have demonstrated knowledge about alcoholism and freedom to let the drinking be the drinker's problem, even to let the person continue to drink if alcoholism is present.

The spouse or other family member may have some questions or concerns about such a test. He or she may think it's a waste of time and the person needs to get help. This then becomes a judgment call. If you definitely think it would still be a good idea, you can indicate your understanding of why he or she would feel that way, but also express your reasons why you think the test may be an appropriate next step. If this is to be tried, it is important to talk with the spouse in front of the alcoholic about the need for him or her to back off on the drinking during this period of time. Such understanding surprises the alcoholic and enhances the relationship with the pastor. This kind of conversation in the presence of the person whose drinking is in question can be very helpful again in assuring that if the test is taken and failed, the person will seek a professional evaluation.

The following questions can also help you identify alcoholism:

- Do you lose time from work due to drinking?
- Is drinking making your home life unhappy?
- Do you drink because you are shy with other people?
- Is drinking affecting your reputation?
- Have you ever felt remorse after drinking?
- Have you gotten into financial difficulties as a result of drinking?
- Does your drinking make you careless of your family's welfare?
- Has your ambition decreased since drinking?
- Do you crave a drink at a definite time daily?
- Do you want a drink the next morning?
- Does drinking cause you to have difficulty in sleeping?
- Has your efficiency decreased since drinking?
- Is drinking jeopardizing your job or business?
- Do you drink to escape from worries or trouble?
- Do you drink alone?

- Have you ever had a complete loss of memory as a result of drinking?

- Has your physician ever treated you for drinking?

- Do you drink to build up your self-confidence?

- Have you ever been to a hospital or treatment facility because of drinking?

Three yes answers usually means the drinking is alcoholism. Four yes answers means the drinking is definitely alcoholism. Either result requires a professional assessment.

The time may come when all efforts have failed in getting the person to seek professional help. Then you need to talk with the spouse and other family members about scheduling an appointment with professional staff at an alcoholism services facility to plan for an intervention. Frequently, after necessary planning, an intervention can be the event and process that moves the person into treatment. (Chapter 14 describes intervention in detail.)

## FOURTH- AND FIFTH-STEP WORK

One special service you can offer members of your parish and others in the community is to provide assistance with Step Four and Step Five of the Twelve Steps. You can reread the section on these steps in the Big Book of Alcoholics Anonymous.[1] A fourth-Step inventory guide written by Carl Anderson will give you a better idea of how the fourth Step is done, as well as the basic content.[2] Keep a supply to give to alcoholics for their own use. Treatment facilities can provide special orientation and training. Some have ongoing programs to train clergy in the community to do fifth-Step work with their patients.

Providing guidance for writing the fourth-Step inventory and being available to listen to fifth Steps provides opportunity for spiritual counsel and guidance. It is important for members of your congregation to know that you are available for such a service and that you are also free *to have them do this with someone else*. Some prefer not to do this with their own pastor.

The reason for Steps Four and Five can be gained from AA literature, particularly the Big Book, *Alcoholics Anonymous*.[3] Emphasize the need to be as honest as possible in the written inventory. Talk about the inventory in a positive manner as a way to get to know oneself better; to identify that which most bothers one and about which there is the greatest guilt; to identify character defects that require change and strengths that need to be affirmed; to identify what in the inventory can serve as danger signals that can lead to drinking again.

The assumption is that the defects listed in the fourth-Step inventory guide are present in some form or other. You will see that the list includes selfishness, alibis, pride, resentments, dishonest thinking, phoniness, and self-pity. It may be difficult to identify and affirm gifts and strengths until there has been some sobriety with responsible behavior. Nevertheless, the importance of this part of an inventory needs to be underscored.

When scheduling a fifth Step, allow sufficient time so there will be no sense of hurry. Ninety minutes ought to be enough. Provide for no interruptions except for extreme emergencies. Arrange for a comfortable environment and give assurance of absolute confidentiality with your undivided attention. Initial nervousness can be handled by some casual conversation. You may indicate that you will be taking notes for discussion, but will tear them up and throw them away. Do that in the presence of the person at the conclusion of Step Five. The emphasis is on listening. Ask questions only for clarification or expansion. What may appear to be a big thing with the person may appear to be a little thing to you.

There can be a great deal of variation in the nature and quality of the content of the inventory and the way it is communicated. Some will clearly not have made good preparation. This needs to be noted and discussed. Maybe the person isn't ready yet for these steps, but an initial effort needs to be commended with consideration for another later on. Maybe it is the best the person is able to do. Sometimes by taking the lead the pastor can help the person to better see and express what is there or possibly left out. If there are some indicators that the person isn't really prepared and is doing this out of compliance, the question needs to be raised and discussed. As long as the pastor is open and honest, no harm will be done. Throughout Step Five the person needs to be allowed to experience the inherent pain in anything that has been included.

During Step Five resentments may arise that have been identified but not worked through; guilt may be expressed but still be a burden. You need to provide counsel for certain acts of behavior that need to be addressed and for making amendment with those who have been wronged and hurt, including self.

Once you and the person have completed Step Five, you may wish to ask, "Having done this now, taken this kind of look at yourself, how do you feel about yourself?" This can lead into some key areas for pastoral counseling. If the person has grown up in the church and indicates belief in God, you can reflect, "How do you think God feels about you as you look at all this?" The person may gain a fresh understanding of God's grace. Key biblical passages learned in childhood can be given new meaning. If the person hasn't been reared in the church or has become an agnostic, discuss how he or she perceives a Higher Power. Asking for help in the morning and expressing gratitude in the evening can be appropriate actions.

It is always good to mention that the person may decide later to do another fourth and fifth Step. In some situations you may recommend that this be done again after a lengthier period of sobriety.

If you have any questions about anything after taking Step Five, talk with a pastor on the staff of a treatment program, or one you know who has more experience.

## SOME OTHER QUESTIONS

What about prayer and meditation with the alcoholic and family members? Many alcoholics and family members have used prayer, and there can be value in exploring the content of the prayers. Some recovering alcoholics talk about having used prayer to fool themselves into believing that they really wanted to quit drinking when they weren't really ready yet, because either they didn't understand what alcoholism was or weren't ready to seek outside help. Frequently, family members have prayed for the alcoholic to stop drinking, not for learning how they can get help and change their own patterns. They also need to know from you that prayer in and of itself is not sufficient. *Action needs to be taken.*

If you pray with them, do what is comfortable in your ministry and what you think would be meaningful to the alcoholic and family members. Your prayer can help to focus on "what is and needs to be." There can be value in your sharing the Serenity Prayer: "God, grant me the serenity to accept the things I cannot change, courage to change the things I can, and wisdom to know the difference."

What about private, religious confession? This requires careful discernment, and the pastor must be certain that he or she is not imposing a personal agenda onto the person. For some, given their religious tradition and previous involvement in worship, formal private confession may be helpful after completion of Step Five. If you think so but have reservations, ask the person, and make clear that it is not part of Step Five.

You will need to decide whether prayer would be appropriate at the end of the fifth-Step session. You can determine this within the context of your own practice and where you think the person is. There can be two rules: (1) If it is natural for you to pray at such a time, you can do that—but make sure you are not laying religious language or doctrinal statements on the person that are not part of his or her personal beliefs; (2) ask the person if he or she would like you to have a prayer. The Serenity Prayer by itself or included in a larger prayer can always be appropriate for any person in AA or Al-Anon.

Helping people take Steps Four and Five can result in some new personal awareness and reflection on the implications for confession within the life of the church.

What about wine? A longstanding question has been the wisdom of partaking of wine in the Lord's Supper when that is the practice in the person's church. I once heard a recovering Episcopalian priest say, "If an alcoholic takes wine in the Eucharist and gets drunk, he was already headed for a drink." My counsel is that this is the one place—and the amount can be very limited—where a recovering alcoholic can take wine without jeopardy. The purpose is completely different. The context is spiritual and Christ-centered. I know of none who have done this who then got drunk. It is significant to note that this is the only time, place, and situation where I know an alcoholic can safely partake of even the smallest amount of alcohol. This can also be an expression of ultimate trust in the Lord.

Some say that is putting too much emphasis on the wine in the Lord's Supper. Personally, I am not so sure of that but recognize that it is a debatable subject. Some alcoholics reared in such a religious tradition ask for grape juice. In one congregation it is announced in the bulletin that the glasses in the middle of the tray are grape juice. If I were a parish pastor, I would explore and discuss this matter fully with recovering alcoholics.

It is important to let all people in your congregation or community know that you are available to provide counseling on any spiritual issues that may arise along the way, or for listening and referral for any other problems that may surface. It is predictable that as you go with some of these people in their pain and also in their spiritual recovery, your life and faith will be enriched.

# 14. Intervention

Most alcoholics enter treatment programs or AA because of some kind of pressure or intervention. It is not necessary or advisable to wait until the alcoholic wants help. Intentional intervention is an essential expression of loving, caring, and helping.

## INFORMAL INTERVENTION

Intervention is not a singular event. What is commonly known as "doing an intervention" is identified in this chapter as Intervention. However, there are other forms of intervention.

The education that you do as a pastor and that a congregational Support Team Ministry does are forms of intervention. Congregations provide a positive environment of understanding, acceptance, and concern, and more family members will be motivated to seek help.

Your first contact and ongoing relationship with the family members or alcoholic are initial interventions. It is to be hoped that the family members will then go for their own assessment or engage in family treatment services and Al-Anon. Even if the alcoholic refuses to see you, a nonmoralistic, caring message from you has been heard by the alcoholic through the spouse. That is a positive intervention. If the alcoholic does see you but refuses to go for professional assessment or to AA, you have established a nonmoralistic relationship, shared key information on "loss of control" and the progressive nature of alcoholism, and in the process spoiled the drinking. No longer is the question one of being able to take it or leave it, but rather being able to take it and control it. The primary focus has been put where it needs to be: on the drinking. That is a positive intervention.

If the family members go for help, that clearly is an intervention. If they benefit from the help, they will be able to practice detachment and nonmoralistically let the alcoholic be responsible for the drinking, the resultant behaviors, and the natural consequences. That clearly is positive intervention. When the spouse, finally without resentment or recrimination, decides the alcoholic has to choose between the marriage and the drinking, that is intervention.

When the employer recommends professional assessment and recommendations, together with the clear message that there has to be improvement in job performance, that is intervention.

When the physician identifies the symptomatology of alcoholism and recommends further assessment or treatment, that is intervention.

A diagnosis of alcoholism by a mental health professional or the recommendation that the person be referred to an alcoholism treatment facility is also an intervention.

When the person, as a result of nonmoralistic concerned pressure, agrees to have an assessment or enter treatment, that is an effective intervention, but sometimes continuing pressure is needed as a continuing intervention. Here are three successful examples:

- Don reluctantly agreed to an assessment. The diagnosis was alcoholism. Don continued to deny his drinking problem and need for treatment. The physician was called in. He stressed the medical aspects as well as the clinical indicators of alcoholism and recommended a blood work-up. Don agreed to have blood drawn. In the return visit the physician shared the results, which clearly indicated acute liver damage that would get worse and strongly recommended treatment. Don wouldn't agree to the full inpatient program, but did agree to give it a try. He stayed for the entire program, found AA, and began recovery.

- Alice was driven from Iowa to Illinois by her husband and one of her sons to be reluctantly admitted to a treatment program because she still didn't believe she had a drinking problem. Her husband and son were certain she would stay, so they returned home. In the detoxification and assessment unit, however, she refused to enter the full treatment program. A son who lived in the area was called in. He said that she was brought there because she needed the full treatment program. She remained adamant in her refusal. The husband and other son were called and made a return trip. Husband and both sons were firm in their confrontation with her to enter the full program. Reluctantly, and with a good deal of resentment, she did.

Within a week Alice was actively participating in the program. She indeed was where she needed to be. Her denial was dissolved. When asked by the staff person involved in the detoxification and assessment unit how things were going, she replied with a smile, "Real good." When seen on her day of discharge, the same staff person was wishing her well and said, "That was a lot of pressure up front from your husband and sons." She replied, *"That was a lot of caring."* The following week her friend was admitted on her recommendation.

- Roger, an upper-management person, entered the detoxification and assessment unit under company pressure. He refused the recommendation for the full treatment program. Roger's vice president and the employee assistance person came out on request of the staff. The employee assistance person expressed the hope that Roger would enter the program. The vice president said he was there *to make sure that he did,* and he did.

## FORMAL INTERVENTION

When these kinds of interventions haven't been effective, or at any time the assessment person recommends, a formal, structured Intervention needs to be done. Some of these Interventions have been done in a harsh, insensitive, inappropriate, manipulative manner in which the persons feel discounted, demeaned, and overly manipulated and the other participants feel used. Such procedures result in damaging hurt, and unnecessary resentment, even if the alcoholic agrees to treatment. One man said, "It got me into treatment and recovery, but also resulted in the deepest and most difficult resentment in my recovery. It was not the way to do it." But this kind of intervention done well is 85 percent to 90 percent effective. Most alcoholism treatment programs provide this kind of intervention with the required pretraining for family members and significant others.

Molly Miller, is someone whom I regard to be an excellent interventionist. She recommends the following steps leading to Intervention, which come from my interview with her.

## Initial Call

The initial phone call with the interventionist is key to a successful intervention. The interventionist speaks as an experienced and understanding, caring, competent, and skillful person. An initial relationship and motivation to pursue intervention need to be established. Basic information is gained over the phone so that the interventionist can already be involved in an initial assessment process. Is it only alcohol, or are other drugs involved? What is it about the drinking that led to this call? Who within the immediate and extended family, possibly including close friends and employers, are concerned about the drinking? Who can come for initial interview? Are there any obvious health problems? Any previous medical treatment or medical emergencies?

In the phone call the interventionist is also seeking: (1) to engage the calling person in the procedure by identifying and affirming fears; (2) to help relieve some of the fears; (3) to provide a brief overview of what will be done; (4) to affirm that the person is doing the right thing; (5) to state that the first step is to just come in and talk.

When Molly is asked if she wants the pastor involved, and is assured that the pastor's input would be meaningful, she responds, "Yes, if at all possible. The pastor can be a positive authority figure in affirmation that this is the necessary and right thing to do, and he or she can also be a gentle person who can help provide firmness and stability."

## Planning and Evaluation Session

The initial session is for preliminary planning and evaluation. It is scheduled as soon as possible, with as many significant others who can possibly attend. Through this process the interventionist sets a clear direction but needs to remain flexible and adaptable. If, for instance, the family member thinks the person with the drinking problem would be willing to come to the initial session, or if the person might be willing to come in as a follow-up to the initial session, a meeting is scheduled and the intervention may not be needed. An evaluation, diagnosis, and recommendation would then be made at that session and could well be accepted, even if reluctantly.

The interventionist may recommend a more extensive evaluation, including medical, psychiatric, and psychological assessment that results in entering the recommended level of service for treatment within either a primary outpatient or inpatient program. If the person refuses any of these recommendations, the family needs to proceed toward an Intervention.

The initial planning session for an Intervention may last up to two hours. A more complete drinking history is taken, and discussion follows to find the best place for the Intervention, and to help determine the appropriate level of treatment service. Information is shared on the disease concept to enlarge their understanding of alcoholism, answer any questions, and discuss any denial. Inquiry is made regarding any kind of previous help family members might have received, such as Al-Anon or any family service program. Has the person with the drinking problem received any previous treatment? Information is shared on why the family members need to get help for themselves, and recommendations are made.

Having described how families and individual family members naturally tend to react to the alcoholic and alcoholism, the interventionist inquires about individual reactions and roles (who is the hero, mascot, scapegoat, and other roles identified in the chapter on the family). Identification is made of the family member who is most involved in control issues and behaviors. The interventionist will want this person to become an ally and the person who mobilizes and keeps in touch with the other members of "the team," which is the term used for those who will participate in the Intervention. An ideal team includes six to ten people.

The actual time between the preliminary/planning session and the Intervention may be two to three weeks. Some members of the team may be coming from out of town. Others may have to get time off from work. Insurance coverage for the treatment program needs to be checked. If there is no coverage, the possibility of self-pay over time needs to be explored. If neither is possible, other treatment resources for those without funds need to be explored. The interventionist will assure some kind of adequate treatment resource.

The date for the Intervention should be set at the initial planning session. If the situation seems too problematic, the interventionist may have them come back for a second planning and evaluation session before scheduling the training session.

## Intervention Training

The controller-ally member of the team will make the contacts. Each person is told of the need to make this Intervention a high priority and, if at all possible, to plan to attend. This training session may last up to seven hours.

It is a good idea to have coffee, tea, rolls, and fruit. Eating helps to enhance the social environment in which the training will be done, and helps the team to bond.

There will be about forty-five minutes of process, which includes discussing how each member feels about being there; further elaboration on the disease concept; dealing with resistance, denial, and conflicts; getting specific story information from each one on their personal experiences of the drinking problem; describing again the family illness, reactions, and behaviors; and providing rationale for their need to get help for themselves. If any untreated adult children of alcoholics are on the team, their situation is discussed and recommendations are made.

At an appropriate time the question is raised as to whether or not anyone on the team is concerned about the drinking of any other member. Their concerns are explored and discussed.

This information sharing helps the team members understand that their experiences, reactions, and behaviors in relationship to the drinking problem are similar to those of the person with the drinking problem. They are told what the interventionist will say during the Intervention and in response to any reactions by the person with the drinking problem, including denial, resistance, questions cost, insurance, or job, and refusal to enter treatment. Objections will be met with direct responses.

The question of how to get the person to the Intervention is addressed. The interventionist makes it very clear that *there will be no lying* to the person. However, it is also made clear that *there has to be and will be needed and appropriate manipulation*. The interventionist explains that this will be uncomfortable for them, but the stakes are high and they won't have to endure the discomfort too long. The interventionist will also handle any reactions of the alcoholic to the manipulation.

Each member of the team is asked to write a letter to the alcoholic. They are told that the first thing to write is, "I love you. This is painful for me to write, but I care about you enough to do it." If a team member does not find it appropriate to say, "I love you," he or she is asked to reach down deep below the anger to the love that is there. Team members who are unable to identify any good times in the past are asked to write what they wish they could have been.

Each one is to write specific information on personal painful experiences caused by the drinking and behaviors. The number of incidents and experiences to be included in the letters is decided by the interventionist. They are told to end their letters with, "I love you," and maybe, "I am fearful for your life because of your drinking." The letter can end with, "I am asking you to get treatment today" (not *telling* but *asking*). During the Intervention these letters will be read to the problem drinker.

Here are some examples of what kind of letter might be written:

- Dad, I love you very much. I am concerned about your drinking, what it is doing to you, to me, and other members of our family. You do things that hurt you and others that you wouldn't do if you weren't drinking. Remember when you promised me that you would be at the play in which I had the lead and you didn't make it because you were drinking? That hurt me very deeply. I know you wanted to be there and would have been there if you hadn't been drinking. Dad, I love you. I am concerned about your drinking. I want you to get help.

- Ron, I do love you. Your drinking is causing real and increasing problems. There have been many embarrassing and hurtful experiences because of your drinking. You will remember that you didn't remember what you did at Bill's birthday party and how terrible you felt when I told you. You embarrassed me and everyone else by being so drunk and so loud and really spoiling his party. Your hanging all over the other women was terribly embarrassing for me and all of them. That isn't the first time that has happened. Then Bill tried to get the keys for the car from you so you wouldn't drive home. You refused. He drove me home. Fortunately, you got home okay, but you drove the car right up on the lawn. The next day you told me you didn't remember any of that. Ron, you need help and I want you to get help for your drinking.

- Mother, I love you very much. For many years you and I had something special. But your drinking has caused real hurt and created real problems in our relationship. Remember when we planned an overnight for my friends after the basketball game last month? When we came home, you were drunk, talking silly, and staggering. I was hurt, embarrassed, and angry. My friends were embarrassed. Mother, you need help for your drinking problem. I am very concerned. I want you to get help. I do love you.

- Jan, you are a valued employee. You have had an excellent work record until two years ago. Since then, your job performance has deteriorated. I have talked to you about that and told you specifically how it has deteriorated. I have asked you twice to get an assessment. You refused saying that you were sure your job performance would improve. It hasn't. I don't want to terminate you. I want you to get help for your drinking. You are not only a valued employee, I also care about you. The company expects you to get help.

Notice that the words "alcoholic" and "alcoholism" are not used, but the focus is clearly kept on alcohol, the drinking, and related behaviors. The letters present overwhelming evidence that the problem is alcohol.

The letters should contain no moralistic judgmental statements. The interventionist reads each letter to remove or revise any such statements. She or he also decides who will read first, middle, and last based on the strength they and their letters bring to the Intervention.

The interventionist discusses how the team will handle a possible refusal to accept treatment. They are to respond to a refusal by asking, "Are you saying no?" If so, each member of the team needs to know that and stay firm in stating the consequences. Consequences might be, "Until you get treatment, I can no longer stand by you. I won't be in a relationship with you. You will have to live alone with your drinking."

The interventionist needs to be flexible in scheduling the time and place for the Intervention. Molly says that she has never had an Intervention scheduled and not had the person with the drinking problem present.

The day or evening before the Intervention, the appropriate designated member of the team, usually the spouse, will say to the person with the drinking problem, "I have had some concerns about the children and have been to see a counselor. The counselor wants to see both of us tomorrow." Molly says that it is predictable that the person with the drinking problem will agree to come, with very few exceptions.

On the day of the Intervention, if it is held at the treatment center or the interventionist's office, the other members of the team arrive early and are in a room sitting in a circle. Molly chooses to be near the receptionist's desk when the person with the drinking problem and spouse or other designated team members arrive. She greets the spouse, introduces herself to the alcoholic, and expresses gratitude for his or her willingness to come in.

The alcoholic is usually surprised and shocked. Molly says, "It is a moment of vulnerability which the interventionist wants to use therapeutically." Molly asks the alcoholic to sit next to her, and she sits by the door in case the alcoholic makes a move to leave. The alcoholic rarely leaves.

The interventionist, not the team members, handles any reaction by the alcoholic. The interventionist expresses understanding and acceptance if the alcoholic expresses any feelings of shock, of having not been told the whole truth, or of being manipulated. Then the interventionist says, "Your family and every-one here *really care about you* and are *concerned about you*. They are asking you to listen to them. *Are you willing to do that?"*

All are asked to read their letters. If the alcoholic begins to react with anger, denial, or defensiveness, the interventionist says, "You said you would listen. Are you willing to do that?"

When the Intervention is completed and the person has agreed, perhaps reluctantly, to enter treatment, Molly stands up, steps aside, and says, "Why don't you all give him or her a hug and say again, 'I love you?'" Then the interventionist says, "Who would you like to go with you to the admitting office?"

## CASE HISTORIES

Let's look at a few case histories of Interventions. Although each Intervention will be unique, these stories will give you a feel for what can happen.

### Joan

Joan is thirty-five years of age, single, and very successful in her own business. She is addicted to cocaine as her primary drug of choice, and also uses alcohol and marijuana. She started using cocaine six years ago and has been free-basing for the last three years. Her use of alcohol and marijuana has decreased during this time. Joan recently passed out at work, which scared her boyfriend, Tom.

Tom made the initial call to the interventionist. Because of the urgency of the situation, the initial session became the planning/training session. Tom, a best female friend, and another male friend attended. Tom and Joan have been involved in their relationship for seven years. He has been reluctant to confront her before because the change had been so gradual. He has also used cocaine with her at times, but is not addicted. He is successful in his own business, and has bailed Joan out financially several times.

Mary, Joan's best friend, has been concerned about Joan for the last three or four years because of her increased use of cocaine, her free-basing, and the fact that she has lost about fifteen pounds in the last eight months. Joan has also been isolating herself more.

Joe, a friend and colleague, is aware of a number of times when she was impaired at work. He is into his own recovery and afraid for her life.

Joan has two older sisters, both of whom have been concerned and supported the planning for the Intervention but were unable to attend.

The three friends expressed a lot of anger and guilt during the planning session. They knew they needed to be there, but didn't really want to be there. The interventionist told them that the reason the session was scheduled so quickly was because of the fear that Joan might overdose. They wanted to know about the interventionist's qualifications, the quality of the treatment program, and how she knew this was a disease. They probably had difficulty accepting the disease idea because of their own drug use. The interventionist responded to their belligerence and uncooperativeness by saying that they either had to agree to cooperate and get the Intervention done or stop the whole process. They agreed to cooperate. The interventionist also explained why treatment for cocaine addiction is long and arduous. The letter writing was very difficult, but it was done.

Tom agreed to bring Joan to the Intervention. She had been using cocaine that morning. Usually an Intervention isn't done under those circumstances, but the interventionist decided to proceed because of the urgency of the situation and Joan's apparent physical deterioration.

Joan listened to the letters, refused treatment, and got up to leave. Tom blocked the door. Joan sat down. Further attempts were made to motivate her around her strengths and obvious evidences of her need for help. This went on for about forty-five minutes.

Joan finally agreed to enter treatment, with the qualification that she could call her lawyer the next day. The team didn't have to state consequences. They all gave her big hugs.

After Joan's acceptance and admission to the treatment programs, the interventionist spent time with the team members to address their individual needs for help and make recommendations.

Joan never made the call to her attorney. She not only completed the full inpatient program, but also entered the intensive continuing-care program.

### Richard

Richard is a corporate partner. His wife, Nancy, knew that he had a serious drinking problem. Previously, he had refused inpatient treatment. Nancy was aware that Richard's business partners were going to force his retirement because of his drinking.

Nancy made the initial call and came in for the initial evaluation. The training and Intervention would include their children, other family members, and some of Richard's partners.

Training was very difficult. None of the partners trusted the interventionist, and they challenged the disease concept. Later, over coffee and rolls, the group began to come together for accomplishing the Intervention. The letters by the partners were businesslike, which was appropriate for them. One team member evidenced vulnerability because of the loss of his wife from alcoholism. The partners stated some consequences if Richard refused treatment, but his family did not. They are very comfortable financially, and Nancy has decided to put none of that at risk by stating that she would not leave him if he didn't quit drinking.

Richard refused treatment. He was then told that a report to his company would declare him incompetent. He grudgingly agreed to enter treatment and not drink while in treatment, but said that he wouldn't quit drinking and would voluntarily retire.

This Intervention was not completely successful for Richard, but there is some good news. Nancy did get help for herself and is now volunteering to help other spouses.

### Ruth

Ruth and her husband, Bill, are physicians. Her husband is quite knowledgeable about alcohol addictions and has a nonchemical, untreated addiction of his own. While under the influence of alcohol, Ruth had a car accident in which her car went into a ditch. Fortunately, she wasn't seriously injured. Bill decided that something needed to be done and made the initial call to the interventionist.

Because of the family situation and geographic locations, the preliminary planning session was done only with Bill. He expressed shame because of his wife's drinking problem. He felt they should know better because of their profession. The interventionist talked with other family members on the phone to gather initial information about their knowledge of, experiences with, and concern about Ruth's drinking. The interventionist also provided orientation information on Intervention.

During the training session Bill was very guarded, defensive, and emotionally flat. He had a hard time getting out of his professional role of always being in charge. However, he was very clear on the consequences if Ruth refused treatment. The others did well in the training. It was a very emotional session because of a previous death of a family member from alcoholism. They were very concerned for Ruth's life.

All did a good job of writing their letters. Bill's was quite factual, nonemotional, but usable. The most important thing in his letter was his stated consequence: he would separate from Ruth until she accepted treatment.

The other letters clearly communicated that the writers cared about Ruth and didn't want her to also die because of her drinking.

During the Intervention Ruth stonewalled. She talked about how embarrassing it was for her, and she was rude to the team members. She said they had no right to be there and do this.

They simply listened, shared their love and concern for her, and read their letters.

When Ruth refused treatment, they shared the consequences. Bill was very clear and firm, saying, "I don't think you believe me, but I mean what I have said about separating from you if you refuse treatment."

Ruth still refused.

The interventionist ceased trying to motivate or have the team members motivate Ruth and underscored the recommendation for treatment. Bill was asked to come in for a follow-up interview. He refused.

Failure? It could have been. But three months later Ruth, possibly because of increased knowledge and pain, called for more information on the recommended program, entered treatment, stayed through the full program, and participated in the extensive continuing-care program following primary treatment.

## Clarence

Clarence, an elderly man, had very severe health problems because of his chronic alcoholism. His wife was significantly disabled. Their children live in other communities. Clarence's son, John, received a call from Clarence's friend informing him of his father's deteriorating health. John made the initial call for help.

John came to the evaluation session alone because other members of the family lived farther away, and the need for Intervention was immediate. Clarence had been involved in continuous daily drinking. He had passed out in a number of different places. All previous efforts to get him to seek help had failed.

The training session went very well, with a number of family members and friends involved. All were aware that Clarence's health was precarious and that he would not live long if the drinking continued. They became a very cohesive group, eager to learn, and they accepted their own need for help. Their letters were excellent.

The Intervention was an extremely positive event. They all expressed their love for him together with their real concern and asked if he would get treatment. He agreed to accept treatment. At the end of the Intervention he thanked them all for doing what they did.

This case history is included because Clarence is an elderly person, whose wife is in a nursing home. He could easily have said, "What difference does it make now?" His family and friends could easily have said, "There is no hope. At his age he will just drink himself to death." As long as people who have alcoholism have their mental faculties so that they can comprehend the reality of their condition, there is hope.

# 15. Treatment

Treatment is a process, not a place or an event. The various interventions described in the previous chapter are important parts of that process.

Some alcoholics and family members never enter any professional treatment program, although considerably more do than years ago. They enter AA or Al-Anon by referral from family, pastor, friend, or employer and become involved in recovery. Some try that first and don't make it, because they are not ready yet or because they first need some kind of professional treatment. Others go into professional treatment first and then into AA or Al-Anon. For those who go first to AA or Al-Anon and begin recovery, involvement in a professional outpatient program can significantly enhance their learning and growth.

## PROFESSIONAL ASSESSMENT AND RECOMMENDATIONS

Professional assessment and recommendations are another phase of treatment. The professional will offer the alcoholic and the family a recommendation for treatment, and explain why that level of service is being recommended. If this primary recommendation is refused, then the professional will offer other options, with the hope that the person will accept some level of treatment. The professional should make it clear that if the optional recommendation doesn't work, the alcoholic must then give serious consideration to the primary recommendation.

A good professional assessment will include:

1. Taking a drinking history with inclusion of spouse or significant other and employer representative, if possible.

2. History and physical with a blood work-up that will indicate possible acute or chronic liver damage or other medical conditions caused by the drinking. Such indica-

tors can be used clinically to address denial and establish motivation to get help. If the alcoholic has recently had a history or physical, those results can be used. The physician can then do a diagnosis and begin some intervening.

3. Psychological testing, when indicated, to assess not only psychological impairment but also acute or chronic brain function impairment. Significant results can be used clinically to address denial and establish motivation to get help.

One level of formal treatment is *primary outpatient*. This is more intensive and more highly structured than outpatient counseling, and involves three to four hours in the day or evening several times a week for a number of months. The alcoholic must meet certain criteria to qualify for such a program: first, there must be evidence that the person has been able to stay sober for a period of time; second, there has to be absence of denial or weakened denial, with observable motivation to get some help either because of internal or external pressures. Sometimes a person may be recommended for an inpatient program but will only accept entering a primary outpatient program as the initial step toward help. If this is the case, the person must understand that if the outpatient treatment is not successful, the primary recommendation for the inpatient program will be accepted.

For years *inpatient programs* were described as being three or four weeks. My belief is that most who need inpatient care require a minimum of at least three weeks, and some need longer lengths of stay. However, because of health-care cost containment, people must consider what their insurance covers. Some have to enter inpatient care when they could be in primary outpatient because their insurance only covers inpatient. Whether primary outpatient or inpatient, treatment plans and length of treatment need to be based on the individual's needs.

This book advocates treatment programs that integrate the philosophy and Twelve-Step programs of AA, Al-Anon, and others. Are there any other effective treatment approaches that do not include that philosophy? For years there has been *aversion treatment*, which was once known as the Keeley cure. Medication is given to create an aversion reaction to alcohol, which results in the person getting sick and vomiting. This is a conditioning technique. Some people have stayed sober as a result of this type of treatment. If there is no internal change in philosophy and way of life, however, much of the richness and blessing that occurs in the spiritual recovery programs can be missed. The conditioning effect can also run its course, requiring another conditioning treatment or resulting in resumption of drinking. In recent times some proponents of this kind of treatment have added other components, including referral to AA and Al-Anon.

*Psychoanalysis* or other treatment approaches that consider alcoholism as primarily symptomatic of an underlying disorder have failed. Both therapist and alcoholic live with the delusion that they are really doing something about the problem, frequently at significant financial cost to the patient or insurance carrier. The alcoholism remains untreated, because of the primary diagnosis being depression, anxiety reaction, neurotic disorder, character disorder, and so on.

*Antabuse* treatment has been in existence for some time. This is different than aversion therapy in that alcohol is prohibitive when using Antabuse. People on this daily medication who drink become very ill and need emergency medical treatment. Usually, when Antabuse is prescribed today, it is viewed as supportive therapy together with professional treatment and AA, particularly for those who have been unable to establish any significant time of sobriety. My sense is that Antabuse is being used much less than was the case some years ago.

Some people have recovered through a *religious conversion* experience. There are Christian denominations and pastors who maintain that as the only approach to genuine recovery.

Then there is what appears to be *spontaneous remission*. This rarely happens. The alcoholic—not just a problem drinker—quits drinking and the compulsion is gone for life. You may know such a person. This happened with an uncle of mine. Remembering the severity of his alcoholism, when I heard the news that he had quit drinking, I said, "It can't be. It won't last if he doesn't get outside help. If he stays sober, he will be miserable to live with and very likely develop some serious health problems, such as depression or gastro-intestinal disorder from trying to fight something he can't lick. It's like putting a plug in the tea kettle and setting it on the stove. Something will pop." More than twenty years passed, and none of that happened. He stayed sober until his death. My aunt would tell you that she never dreamed they could have such a good life together.

I don't understand it and don't know anybody who does. Such spontaneous remission is a rare occurrence. I can identify with it because the same thing happened to me with my nicotine addiction. In spite of many efforts over a lengthy period of time to quit smoking on my own, I was never able to quit. One Christmas morning I awoke, didn't want a cigarette, and haven't ever wanted one since. I don't understand it, but I am grateful.

Aftercare or continuing care following primary outpatient or inpatient treatment is extremely important. This is always recommended together with involvement in AA, Al-Anon, or other Twelve-Step groups. There is considerable evidence to support the fact that recovery rates go from 40 percent or 45 percent to 75 percent or 80 percent for those who accept both of these recommendations and complete the aftercare programs. The pastor needs to strongly support recommendations for aftercare.

## COCAINE

A special word needs to be said on cocaine, crack, and cocaine treatment. Cocaine is a stimulant, not a depressant like alcohol. The "high" experience is different, much more intense and immediate. Alcohol and other drugs are frequently involved, but for cocaine addicts, cocaine is the drug of choice. Cocaine patients tend to have a high energy level, a feeling of uniqueness, and denial of other addictions. They are extremely talkative, to the point where that becomes a treatment issue. That they are addicted to an illegal drug brings with it certain special problems and complications. There is also an intense craving for cocaine that can be associated with people, places, smells, feeling states, and sight of drug-related paraphernalia.

All of this means that although there are some basic similarities to other common drug addictions, there are also some basic differences. Based on current experience, cocaine addiction is best treated in either a separate treatment program or in an alcoholism treatment program with a special concentrated cocaine treatment track.

The early results of treatment of cocaine addicts were dismal. Referral resources were heard to report that there were no recoveries. Some treatment programs know much more now than they did in the beginning, and are producing some promising results. Cocaine Anonymous is beginning to experience continuing recovery with more members, so that there is more sustaining support available within the fellowship for new members. If you have a church member with cocaine addiction, seek out special information for the best cocaine treatment programs.

## FINDING A TREATMENT PROGRAM

The human environment is an essential part of treatment and recovery. The "human environment of spirituality" is the nonmoralistic environment in which open but not harsh confrontation is provided by staff and patients to help break down denial and other defensive mechanisms that block the alcoholic or family members from accepting the illness and their need for outside help. This environment includes not only the help of the professional treatment team in the structured program, but the mutual identification, understanding, acceptance, confrontation, and support of the patients and recovering volunteers. There is the clear message that help is needed, help is available, and there is hope.

If you are not familiar with treatment centers in your area, you can check the Yellow Pages for alcoholism assessment and treatment services. If there is more than one treatment facility or outpatient services office, you will need to make your own assessment as to which you think provide quality services or inquire from other people whose judgment you respect. Your regular telephone book will also provide listings for AA and other Twelve-Step groups.

To determine the quality of services in a particular program, you must ask the following questions:

1. Do they see alcoholism as the primary problem and recommend direct treatment of the alcoholism, or do they

see alcoholism as symptomatic of an underlying psychiatric or psychological condition?

2. Do the treatment services have the philosophy and Twelve Steps of Alcoholics Anonymous, Al-Anon, and other similar Twelve-Step groups integrated into their program, with a clear, strong focus on the spiritual aspects of recovery?

3. Do they have volunteers actively involved in an AA and other Twelve-Step groups?

4. Is the facility accredited by the Joint Commission on Accreditation of Hospitals, which includes the accreditation of alcoholism-treatment facilities and services?

5. Does their counseling staff include recovering people active in the appropriate Twelve-Step groups together with M.A. and Ph.D. clinicians, trained and experienced in alcoholism treatment, who understand and accept the spiritual recovery programs?

6. Do they have full-time or part-time staff qualified to provide medical, psychiatric, and psychological services who believe alcoholism is a disease needing direct treatment? Does this staff positively affirm the various Twelve-Step groups?

7. Do they have a holistic approach that requires interdisciplinary teamwork?

8. Do they refrain from using mood-altering drugs following detoxification during primary and continuing-care treatment?

9. Do they have a comprehensive services system, or have access to such a system, that includes: assessments; primary outpatient; residential and hospital levels of inpatient treatment; continuing care following primary treatment; family programs; specialty programs for certain groups of patients, such as older adults, relapsers, and youth?

10. Do they provide or have access to a concurrent dual-illness treatment service for those alcoholics who have

serious medical/psychiatric conditions and eating disorders? In such a program do they use needed and appropriate medications for patients with psychiatric disorders,
which enhance the possibility for recovery?

11. Do they have individual and group counseling?

12. Do they welcome and encourage the pastor's interest and
    appropriate involvement and provide an opportunity for
    in-service orientation?

13. Do they encourage patients to do initial fourth- and fifth-
    Step work in primary treatment?

14. Do they provide Intervention?

15. Do they have credible outcome studies?

It may be that no facility in your area meets all of these criteria,
and you will have to decide whether the facility has enough to
assure quality treatment. As with many other situations, you do
the best with what is available. However, if the services available
are seriously lacking in quality, consider using treatment services
outside the area.

In all that is done with and for the alcoholic and the family, in
all that is received by and from the alcoholic and the family, we
experience again the grace of God within community.

# Notes

## Preface

1. Institute of Social Research: University of Michigan, 1988 and National Institute on Drug Abuse: Rockville, Maryland, 1987.

## 2. Progressive Symptoms of Alcoholism

1. E. M. Jellinek, *The Disease Concept of Alcoholism* (New Brunswick, NJ: Hillhouse Press, 1972).
2. Ibid.
3. Ibid.
4. Jellinek, pp. 36–41. If we add the current knowledge related to possible genetic factors in some alcoholism, Jellinek's identifications and descriptions remain valid and valuable.

## 4. The Spiritual Recovery Program of Alcoholics Anonymous

1. *Alcoholics Anonymous Comes of Age* (New York: Alcoholics Anonymous World Services, Inc., 1957), 64.
2. Ibid., 58–59.
3. Ibid., 63.
4. Ibid., 63–64.
5. *Alcoholics Anonymous* (New York: Alcoholics Anonymous World Services, Inc., 1955), 13.
6. *Alcoholics Anonymous Comes of Age* (New York: Alcoholics Anonymous World Services, Inc., 1957), 161–162.
7. Ibid., 74.
8. Ibid., 39.
9. Ibid., 167.
10. *Alcoholics Anonymous* (New York: Alcoholics Anonymous World Services, Inc., 1955), 74–75.
11. *Alcoholics Anonymous Comes of Age* (New York: Alcoholics Anonymous World Services, Inc., 1957), 79.

## 6. Alcoholism: Moral Weakness or Disease?

1. Lloyd H. Steffen, "Rethinking Drinking, the Moral Context," *The Christian Century*, vol.106 (1 November 1989), 684–686.
2. Traynor v. Turnage, 108 SCT, 1372 (1988).

## 7. Shame and Guilt

1. Ernest Kurtz, *Shame and Guilt: Characteristics of the Dependency Cycle* (Center City, MN: Hazelden Education Materials, 1981).

## 9. Compliance vs. Surrender

1. *Alcoholics Anonymous* (New York: Alcoholics Anonymous World Services, Inc., 1955), 246–251.
2. Ibid.
3. Carl Anderson. Nonpublished material on listings of values and behaviors related to spiritual and nonspiritual being dominant in the book *Alcohlics and Their Families, A Guide for Clergy and Congregations*. New York: Alcoholics Anonymous World Services, Inc.
4. Ibid.

## 10. The Family

1. Ronald W., "Free From Codependency" *Parkside Magazine* (Winter 1989): 20.
2. Joan Jackson, "The Adjustment of the Family to the Crisis of Alcoholism," *Quarterly Journal of Alcohol Studies*, vol. 15, no. 4 (December 1954), 562–586.
3. Betty Reddy, Community Relations, Parkside Lutheran Hospital. Parkside, IL.

## 11. Caring Pastors and Other Helpers

1. *Alcoholics Anonymous* (New York: Alcoholics Anonymous World Services, Inc., 1939).

## 12. Equipping the Congregation

1. *An Elephant in Your Sanctuary*. Merchantville, NJ: Interlink Video Productions, 1990 Film.
2. Roger Svendsen, *Chemical Health* (Chicago, IL: Division for Congregational Life, Evangelical Lutheran Church in America).

## 13. Counseling Alcoholics and Family Members

1. *Alcoholics Anonymous* (New York: Alcoholics Anonymous World Services Inc., 1939), 64–75.
2. Carl Anderson. *Fourth Step Inventory Guide* (Park Ridge, IL: Parkside Publishing Corporation, 1987).
3. *Alcoholics Anonymous* (New York: Alcoholics Anonymous World Services, Inc., 1939), 64–75.

# Additional Resources

## RECOMMENDED READING

### Understanding Alcoholism, Other Addictions, and Recovery

*Al-Anon Family Groups.* New York: Al-Anon Family Groups, 1966.
> This is Al-Anon's basic book like the "Big Book" of AA. Must reading.

*Al-Anon Twelve Steps and Twelve Traditions.* New York: Al-Anon Family Groups, 1953.
> Shares the experience, the strength, and the hope for further self-discovery and personal growth.

*Alateen: Hope for Children of Alcoholics.* New York: Al-Anon Family Groups, 1973.
> The book on the Twelve-Step recovery group for young people.

*Alcoholics Anonymous.* New York: Alcoholics Anonymous World Services, 1939.
> This is AA's original book, called the "Big Book." It includes Bill W.'s story, what AA is, how AA understands alcoholism, how AA works, and in the revised edition, includes the stories of early and later members. Essential reading for learning about AA.

*Alcoholics Anonymous Comes of Age.* New York: Alcoholics Anonymous World Services, 1957.
> The very interesting and valuable inside story of the development of AA, the Twelve Steps and Twelve Traditions, and the three legacies of AA: Recovery, Unity, Service. Ought to be of special interest to clergy.

Anderson, Carl. *Fourth Step Inventory Guide.* Park Ridge, IL: Parkside Publishing Corporation, 1987.
> Recommended for clergy to use as a guide for helping alcoholics and for other recovering people to use in working on their personal inventory.

Apthorp, Stephen P. *Alcoholism and Substance Abuse.* Wilton, CT: Morehouse Barlow, 1985.
> A clergy handbook.

Beattie, Melody. *Codependent No More.* San Francisco: Harper & Row, 1987.
> Defines and describes crippling effects of codependecy and the way to health.

Black, Claudia. *It Will Never Happen to Me.* Denver: Printers and Publications Division, 1982.
One of the definitive works about children of alcoholics.

Clarke, Jean Illsley and Connie Dawson. *Growing Up Again.* San Francisco: Harper & Row, 1989.
Help for learning how to parent, especially if one has been badly parented, thus breaking the cycle.

Ebbitt, Joan. *Tomorrow, Monday or New Years Day: Emerging Issues in Eating Disorders Recovery.* Park Ridge, IL: Parkside Publishing Corporation, 1989.
Addresses conflicts that will emerge in recovery such as self-esteem, sexuality, intimacy, and spirituality and how to deal with these.

Gold, Mark S. *800-Cocaine.* New York: Bantam Books, 1984.
A straightforward, informative, and prescriptive manual for anyone who needs to know about this problem.

Hay, Veronica. *Design For Growth: Twelve Steps For Adult Children.* San Francisco: Harper & Row, 1989.
A fresh approach to the Twelve Steps that offers hope and encouragement, stressing the importance of prayer and affirmations.

Hull-Mast, Nancy and Duane Purcell. *Sibs.* Park Ridge, IL: Parkside Publishing Corporation, 1989.
For the brothers and sisters of alcoholics who are clinically dependent. Explains how they have been affected and how they can get help for themselves.

Johnson. Vernon E. *I'll Quit Tomorrow.* San Francisco: Harper & Row, 1973.
Defines the stages of alcoholism but is most noted for its explanation of the process of intervention by families to help alcoholics.

Keller, John. *Drinking Problem?* Minneapolis: Augsburg Fortress, 1971.
Part of a series for pastors to help them in their counseling, and recommended reading for alcoholics and their families.

_____.*Let Go, Let God.* Augsburg Fortress, 1985.
Alcoholism, AA, and the Twelve Steps are used as a paradigm for understanding basic Christian beliefs regarding our essential human condition, grace, conversion, and new life in the Spirit.

Klausner, Mary Ann and Bobbie Hasselbring. *Aching For Love, The Sexual Drama of the Adult Child, Healing Strategies for Women.* San Francisco: Harper & Row, 1990.
This is the first book to explore the impact that growing up in a dysfunctional family has on a woman's sexuality.

Kurtz, Ernest. *AA: The Story.* San Francisco: Harper & Row, 1979.

The fundamental and first message of AA to its members is that they are not God. Recommended for clergy.

_____. *Shame and Guilt.* Center City, MN: Hazelden Educational Materials, 1981.
Insightful explanation of the difference between shame and guilt that contains the importance of addressing shame with alcoholics and their families. Contains valuable implications for teaching and preaching.

L., Elizabeth. *Keep Coming Back: The Spiritual Journey of Recovery in Overeaters Anonymous.* San Francisco: Harper & Row, 1989.
Discusses highs and lows that accompany ongoing recovery from an eating disorder and provides guidance and tools for maintaining recovery.

Larsen, Earnie. *Old Patterns, New Truths.* San Francisco: Harper & Row, 1988.
A workbook for adult children of alcoholics that shows creative ways of dealing with problems in their past and how they can change current behavior.

_____. *Stage II Recovery: Life Beyond Addiction.* San Francisco: Harper & Row, 1985.
Practical guide on how to see and change learned self-defeating behavior and make relationships work—the core of full recovery.

Lloyd, Roseann and Richard Solly. *Journey Notes: Writing For Recovery and Spiritual Growth.* San Francisco: Harper & Row, 1989.
A guide for anyone who uses writing for reflection and self-discovery and gives those keeping journals in Twelve-Step programs a way of strengthening recovery.

May, Gerald G. *Addiction and Grace.* San Francisco: HarperSanFrancisco, 1991.
Affirms that we are not in control of our lives until we surrender to God.

McFarland, Barbara and Tyeis Baker Baumann. *Feeding the Empty Heart: Adult Children and Compulsive Eating.* San Francisco: Harper & Row, 1988.
Breaks new ground in establishing the connection between eating disorders and family history of compulsive behavior.

Mehl, Duane. *The High Road.* Park Ridge, IL: Parkside Publishing Corporation, 1988.
A library of information on addictions and spiritual breakthroughs. A one-volume treasury of facts and faith.

Mellody, Pia and Andrea Wells Miller. *Breaking Free: A Recovery Workbook For Facing Codependence.* San Francisco: Harper & Row, 1989.

Morreim, Dennis. *Road to Recovery.* Minneapolis: Augsburg Fortress, 1990.

Relates Bible and biblical themes to each of the Twelve Steps of
AA.

*Narcotics Anonymous*. Van Nuys, CA: Narcotics Anonymous World Service, 1982.
Basic text of NA for recovery. Shares experience, strength, and
hope.

O'Gorman, Patricia and Phillip Oliver-Diaz. *Breaking the Cycle of Addiction*. Pompano Beach, FL: Health Commmunications, 1987.
A parent's guide for raising healthy children and breaking the
cycle of addiction from one generation to the next.

*Overeaters Anonymous*. Torrence, CA: Overeaters Anonymous, 1980.
The basic book for Overeaters Anonymous and their program
based on the Twelve Steps.

Parker, Christian. *When Someone You Love Drinks Too Much: A Christian
Guide to Addiction, Codependecy, and Recovery*. San Francisco:
Harper & Row, 1990.
Offers a Christian woman's perspective on what it means to be
married to and cope with an alcoholic. Contains personal expe-
riences and practical advice.

Potter-Efron, Ronald and Patricia Potter-Efron. *Letting Go of Shame*. San
Francisco, Harper & Row, 1989.
Explores nature of shame, reveals its sources, shows its impor-
tant and healthy functions versus excessive, harmful shame.

Reddy, Betty. *A Family Illness*. Park Ridge, IL: Parkside Publishing Corporation, 1987.
Describes effects of alcoholism on the family and provides steps
for positive action and change.

_____and Orville M. McElfresh. *Detachment and Recovery in Family Mem-
bers*. Park Ridge, IL: Parkside Publishing Corporation, 1987.

Smith, Carol Cox. *Recovery At Work*. San Francisco: Harper & Row, 1990.
Helps recovering people see how a job aids or hinders their healing process.

*Staying Clean: Living Without Drugs*. Center City, MN: Hazelden Educational Materials, 1987.
A guide that delves into ideas for staying drug free in practicing
the Twelve Steps of NA.

Svendsen, Roger. *Chemical Health*. Chicago: Division for Congregational
Life, Evangelical Lutheran Church in America, 1986.
An excellent guide for education in congregations regarding ab-
stinence, drinking, other chemical use, alcoholism, response, and
prevention. Contains a theological précis written by Dr. Walter
Wietzke on chemical health.

*Tiebout Papers*. Center City, MN: Hazelden Educational Materials.
"Direct Treatment of a Symptom" (1973).

Dr. Tiebout describes why, as a psychiatrist, he believes alcoholism needs direct treatment versus treatment as a symptomatic disorder.

"The Ego Factors in Surrender" (1954).

An excellent paper that enables clergy and congregations to correlate with their understandings of conversion in the Christian faith.

"Surrender vs. Compliance in Therapy" (1953).

Another excellent paper that can enhance understanding of conversion within the context of the Christian faith.

"The Act of Surrender in the Therapeutic Process" (n.d.).

Dr. Tiebout establishes that there is a psychic event identified as surrender that can enhance understanding of what goes on in the therapeutic process.

*Twelve Steps and Twelve Traditions*. New York: Alcoholics Anonymous World Services, 1953.

Explains the Twelve Steps and covers nature and content of the Twelve Traditions as being vital to preserving the fellowship.

Twerski, Abraham. *Addictive Thinking: Understanding Self-Deception*. San Francisco: Harper & Row, 1990.

How lies we tell ourselves perpetuate addiction.

Wegscheider-Cruse, Sharon, *Choice-Making*. Pompano Beach, FL: Health Communications, 1985.

For codependents, adult children of alcoholics, and spiritual seekers.

Woititz, Janet Geringer. *Struggle for Intimacy*. Pompano Beach, FL: Health Communications, 1985.

For adult children of alcoholics. Deals with learning what a healthy relationship is.

_____. *Adult Children of Alcoholics*. Pompano Beach, FL: Health Communications, 1983.

Identifies thirteen emotional hangups that plague many people who grew up in alcoholic families and how to learn to live with a sense of serenity and freedom.

## Meditation and Devotional Books

*Body, Mind and Spirit*. Park Ridge, Il: Parkside Publishing Corporation, 1990.

One of the best of the new daily meditation books for recovering people.

Keller, Paul F. *God Grant: 365 Christ-Centered Daily Meditations for Recovery*. San Francisco: Harper & Row, 1989.

A Lutheran minister, writing from his own recovery, relates the Twelve Steps to the gospels. Written for those who want more of God's love, Christ's fellowship, and the Holy Spirit's power.

*Our Best Days*. Park Ridge, IL: Parkside Publishing Corporation, 1990.
    Excellent daily meditations for young people in recovery but
    equally of value for adults.

*Touchstones*. Center City, MN: Hazelden Educational Materials, 1986.
    A very good inspirational book of daily meditations for recover-
    ing people.

*Twenty-Four Hours a Day*. Center City, MN: Hazelden Educational Ma-
    terials, 1975.
    The original daily meditation book for recovering people.


## FILM

*An Elephant In Your Sanctuary*. Park Ridge, IL: The Presbyterian Network
on Alcohol and other Drug Abuse and Parkside Publishing Corporation,
1990.

A twenty-eight minute videotape showing examples of congregations
responding to problems of addictions within their congregations and
communities. Very good for education, increasing awareness, and seeing what can be done to make a difference.


## SOURCES

Al-Anon Family Groups, Inc.
P.O. Box 862, Midtown Station
New York, NY 10018-0862

Alcoholics Anonymous World Service
P.O. Box 495, Grand Central Station
New York, NY 10163

Augsburg Fortress Publishers
426 South Fifth Street
Minneapolis, MN 55440

Bantam Books, Inc.
666 Fifth Avenue
New York, NY 10103

Division for Congregational Life
Evangelical Lutheran Church in America
8765 Higgins Road
Chicago, IL 60631-4188

HarperSanFrancisco
Icehouse One—401
151 Union Street
San Francisco, CA 94111-1299

Hazelden Educational Materials
P.O. Box 176
Center City, MN 55012-0176

Health Communications, Inc.
1721 Blount Road
Pompano Beach, FL 33069

Morehouse Barlow, Inc.
78 Danbury Road
Wilton, CT 06897

Narcotics Anonymous World Service, Inc.
P.O. Box 9999
Van Nuys, CA 91409

National Council on Alcoholism and Drug Dependence
12 W. 21st Street — 8th Floor
New York, NY 10010

Overeaters Anonymous, Inc.
4025 Spencer Street, Suite 203
Torrance, CA 90503

Parkside Publishing Corporation
205 West Touhy Avenue
Park Ridge, IL 60068

For further information on available resources you can contact the State Commission on Alcoholism at your state capital and your national church headquarters for any materials or programs they might have.

# Index

Abuse: physical, 17, 90, 92; verbal, 17
Acceptance, 66, 67, 97
ACoA (Adult Children of Alcoholics), 80, 102, 104
Acute effects, 18
Adaptive cell metabolism, 15
Addictions, 24–29, 48
Adult children of alcoholics, 48, 80, 127; pastors as, 80–81, 93, 100; relationships of, 100. *See also* ACoA
Aftercare, 139
Aggressive behavior, 17
Agnostics, 37, 119
Al-Anon, 48, 83, 89, 91, 94, 100, 101, 104, 122, 136
Alateen, 48, 102, 104
Alatots, 93
Alcohol: depressant effect of, 20; gulping of, 14; high tolerance level, 7; increased tissue tolerance level, 13, 15; preoccupation with, 14; sneaking, 13, 16; transforming (euphoric) effect of, 19–21; withdrawal, 15, 16. *See also* Drinking
Alcoholic home, 80
Alcoholics: infantile traits of, 73–74; refusal to seek treatment, 109–10, 122, 127, 130, 132; skid-road, 5, 21, 53, 62; talking about the problem, 90; views on their own drinking, 110–17, 119. *See also* Adult children of alcoholics
Alcoholics Anonymous, 6, 21, 78, 97, 101, 102, 104, 136, 141; church resistance to, 46–47; founding of, 30, 35; Fourth and Fifth Step work, 117–19, 120; General Service Board of, 71; international conventions, 33–34; literature of, 100, 117, 118; spiritual recovery program of, 30–44, 47, 65, 66, 76;

sponsorship, 42; Twelve-Step program, 33, 34–43, 45; Twelve Steps listed, 36; Twelve Traditions, 43–44; Twentieth Anniversary Convention, 71
*Alcoholics Anonymous*, 100, 117, 118
Alcoholism: caused by multiple factors, 7; defined, 1, 5–8; family history of, 7; Gamma, 9, 60; moral problem vs. disease concept of, 50–59, 60, 63, 65; as a primary disease, 45; progressive recovery markers of, 9; progressive symptoms of, 9–18; spontaneous remission of, 138–39; types of (Jellinek), 9; warning signals of, 12–15
Alibi system, 15–16, 68, 70
Aloneness, 18
American Medical Association, 45
Anderson, Carl, 75–77, 117
Anorexia, 28
Antabuse treatment, 138
Atheists, 37
Aversion treatment, 137–38

Beer, 1, 17
Behavioral changes, 16–17, 67, 74
*Bible*, 2, 3, 18, 28, 29, 32, 41, 58, 59, 64, 69, 75
Blackouts, 14, 115
Blame, 82, 83, 90
Blood work-up, 123, 136
Bonhoeffer, Dietrich, 68
Bradley, Dr. Nelson J., 20, 24
Brain damage, 18
Bulimia, 28

Cancer, 55
Car accidents. *See* Driving and drinking
Career, 100, 120, 152, 158. *See also* Job problems and loss
Change, 24, 74